Land Delivery Systems in West African Cities

Land Delivery Systems in West African Cities

The Example of Bamako, Mali

Alain Durand-Lasserve, Maÿlis Durand-Lasserve, and Harris Selod

A copublication of the Agence Française de Développement and the World Bank

Africa Development Forum Series

The Africa Development Forum Series was created in 2009 to focus on issues of significant relevance to Sub-Saharan Africa's social and economic development. Its aim is both to record the state of the art on a specific topic and to contribute to ongoing local, regional, and global policy debates. It is designed specifically to provide practitioners, scholars, and students with the most up-to-date research results while highlighting the promise, challenges, and opportunities that exist on the continent.

The series is sponsored by the Agence Française de Développement and the World Bank. The manuscripts chosen for publication represent the highest quality in each institution and have been selected for their relevance to the development agenda. Working together with a shared sense of mission and interdisciplinary purpose, the two institutions are committed to a common search for new insights and new ways of analyzing the development realities of the Sub-Saharan Africa region.

Advisory Committee Members

Agence Française de Développement
Jean-Yves Grosclaude, Director of Strategy
Alain Henry, Director of Research
Guillaume de Saint Phalle, Head of Research and Publishing Division
Cyrille Bellier, Head of the Economic and Social Research Unit

World Bank
Francisco H. G. Ferreira, Chief Economist, Africa Region
Richard Damania, Lead Economist, Africa Region
Stephen McGroarty, Executive Editor, Publishing and Knowledge Division
Carlos Rossel, Publisher

Sub-Saharan Africa

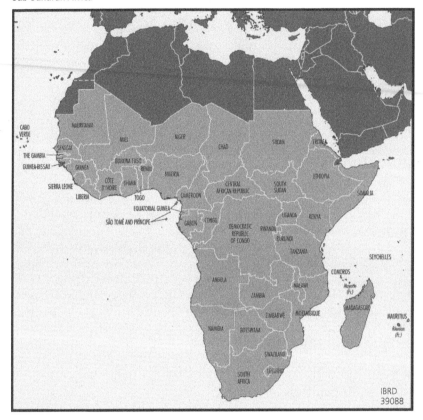

IBRD
39088

Titles in the Africa Development Forum Series

Africa's Infrastructure: A Time for Transformation (2010) edited by Vivien Foster and Cecilia Briceño-Garmendia

Gender Disparities in Africa's Labor Market (2010) edited by Jorge Saba Arbache, Alexandre Kolev, and Ewa Filipiak

Challenges for African Agriculture (2010) edited by Jean-Claude Deveze

Contemporary Migration to South Africa: A Regional Development Issue (2011) edited by Aurelia Segatti and Loren Landau

Light Manufacturing in Africa: Targeted Policies to Enhance Private Investment and Create Jobs (2012) by Hinh T. Dinh, Vincent Palmade, Vandana Chandra, and Frances Cossar

Informal Sector in Francophone Africa: Firm Size, Productivity, and Institutions (2012) by Nancy Benjamin and Ahmadou Aly Mbaye

Financing Africa's Cities: The Imperative of Local Investment (2012) by Thierry Paulais

Structural Transformation and Rural Change Revisited: Challenges for Late Developing Countries in a Globalizing World (2012) by Bruno Losch, Sandrine Fréguin-Gresh, and Eric Thomas White

The Political Economy of Decentralization in Sub-Saharan Africa: A New Implementation Model (2013) edited by Bernard Dafflon and Thierry Madiès

Empowering Women: Legal Rights and Economic Opportunities in Africa (2013) by Mary Hallward-Driemeier and Tazeen Hasan

Enterprising Women: Expanding Economic Opportunities in Africa (2013) by Mary Hallward-Driemeier

Safety Nets in Africa: Effective Mechanisms to Reach the Poor and Most Vulnerable (2015) edited by Carlo del Ninno and Bradford Mills

Urban Labor Markets in Sub-Saharan Africa (2013) edited by Philippe De Vreyer and François Roubaud

Securing Africa's Land for Shared Prosperity: A Program to Scale Up Reforms and Investments (2013) by Frank F. K. Byamugisha

Youth Employment in Sub-Saharan Africa (2014) by Deon Filmer and Louis Fox

Tourism in Africa: Harnessing Tourism for Growth and Improved Livelihoods (2014) by Iain Christie, Eneida Fernandes, Hannah Messerli, and Louise Twining-Ward

All books in the Africa Development Forum series are available for free at
https://openknowledge.worldbank.org/handle/10986/2150

Contents

Boxes

Figures

Maps

Tables

Foreword

The majority of the world's population is now urbanized, and cities continue to grow at a fast pace. In fact, Africa is the continent with the fastest rate of urban growth. As a result of both rural-urban migration as well as natural demographic growth, the urban population in Africa is expected to increase almost threefold, reaching 1.3 billion inhabitants in 2050, more than 500 million of whom will reside in West Africa. Cities can be powerful engines that stimulate trade, facilitate human capital accumulation, foster innovation, and induce structural transformation. As such, this trend of a large and rapid urban population increase could provide an extraordinary opportunity for the growth and economic development of the Africa region.

That said, there is no guarantee that urbanization will drive growth in Africa as it has done elsewhere. In fact, economists have long puzzled over the fact that in some African countries, urbanization could actually be occurring without growth, while not completely understanding why this is so. By focusing on the dysfunctions of the land sector within rapidly expanding West African cities, the authors of this book highlight an important mechanism whereby links between urbanization and growth could be missing, and they shed light on what needs to be done about it.

In West Africa, the rapid pace of city expansion poses a formidable challenge, because the spatial expansion of cities relies predominantly on informal processes to access land for housing, urban services, and infrastructure. One single figure illustrates the scale of the problem: over 60 percent of the urban population in Sub-Saharan African cities are currently living in slums and informal settlements. In turn, the informal expansion of cities creates major difficulties for urban planning, infrastructure provision, and environmental protection. At the core of these challenges is weak land governance—particularly land management and administration—and a malfunctioning land sector. With different land tenure systems coexisting, the procedures to make land available for housing are complex, costly, and nontransparent. Land markets are highly distorted and do not allocate land efficiently. For the majority of the urban population, especially the poor and the middle class, accessing land for housing has become increasingly difficult; holding land is insecure; and conflicts over land are pervasive. These problems exacerbate inequality, threaten social and political stability, and fail to provide the enabling environment for productive investments.

Designing effective policies to address these issues will require an in-depth understanding of the context and political economy of the land sector, notably how land is supplied and accessed. This book provides a new method and analytical framework to assess complex land-delivery systems and land markets, and to identify the necessary interventions in the land sector. Using the example of Bamako, Mali, the analysis sheds light on land-governance issues that are relevant for many other cities in the region as well. We hope that conducting similar systemic diagnoses for other cities, following the method illustrated in this book, can better inform land policies across the region. Addressing land issues will be key to ensuring that urbanization in West Africa contributes to more inclusive growth and shared prosperity, rather than being a missed opportunity.

Makhtar Diop
Vice President
Africa Region
The World Bank Group

Acknowledgments

The authors are indebted to Demba Karagnara for superb research assistance and coordination of the field work; Lamine Camara and his team for contributions to the survey; Lara Tobin for contributions to the statistical analysis and monitoring of the survey of land transfers; and Brian Blankespoor for help with geographic information system programming and mapping. They are also very grateful to Amadou Cissé, Zié Coulibaly, Wim Dekkers, Moussa Djiré, Juliette Paradis-Coulibaly, Fily Bouaré Sissoko, and Christian Vang Eghoff, as well as many informants and "land practitioners" in Mali for their useful discussions. The authors are grateful to two anonymous reviewers for their remarks and suggestions; to the World Bank's Knowledge for Change Program for seminal funding of a broader research program on urbanization under the supervision of Uwe Deichmann; and to the World Bank's Multi-Donor Trust Fund for Sustainable Urban Development for support in the advanced stages of the study.

About the Authors

Alain Durand-Lasserve is emeritus senior research fellow at the Centre National de la Recherche Scientifique (CNRS), France. He is attached to the Laboratory Les Afriques dans le Monde (LAM), a joint research center between the University of Bordeaux, the CNRS, and the National Foundation for Political Sciences, France. He is currently a member of the Technical Committee Land and Development (French Development Agency and Ministry of Foreign Affairs). During the past two decades he has been involved in research and consultancy on land and tenure issues with bilateral cooperation agencies (the U.K. Department for International Development, Deutsche Gesellschaft für Internationale Zusammenarbeit, the Millennium Challenge Corporation, French Cooperation), with multilateral development agencies (UN-Habitat, United Nations Development Programme, Food and Agriculture Organization of the United Nations), and with the World Bank, mainly—but not exclusively—in Sub-Saharan African countries. He has published extensively on tenure formalization and urban land and housing policies.

Maÿlis Durand-Lasserve's background is in economics (University of Paris I). Until her recent retirement, she was professor at the department of sociology at University Victor Segalen of Bordeaux, France, where she taught social history. She is now a consultant with Geoffrey Payne and Associates as an expert on land and tenure policies, especially on the relationships between urban and rural land tenure and tenure formalization in Sub-Saharan African countries.

Harris Selod is a senior economist with the World Bank's Development Research Group. His current work focuses on urban development, transport, and land issues in developing countries, with a specific interest in West Africa. Over the past several years, he has held various positions within the World Bank, including as a visiting scholar to the research department, as a land policy expert seconded by the government of France, and presently as staff.

He has been co-chair of the World Bank's Land Policy and Administration thematic group (2011–13) and co-designed the Land Governance Assessment Framework, a diagnostic tool now implemented in more than 50 countries. Before joining the World Bank in 2007, he was a researcher at the French National Institute for Agricultural Research as well as an associate professor of Economics at the Paris School of Economics (where he taught microeconomic theory and urban studies).

French Acronyms

ACI	Agence de cession immobilière (Land Development Agency)
APIM	Association des promoteurs immobiliers du Mali (Property Developers Association of Mali)
CARPOLE	Cellule de cartographie polyvalente (Mapping Center)
CFAF	CFA franc
CR	*concession rurale* (rural concession)
CRUH	*concession rurale à usage d'habitation* (rural concession for residential purposes)
CUH	*concession urbaine d'habitation* (urban concession for residential purposes)
DDC-DB	Direction des domaines et du cadastre du District de Bamako (Bamako District Directorate of State Domains and of the Land Register)
DNDC	Direction nationale des domaines et du cadastre (National Directorate of State Domains and of the Land Register)
DRDC	Direction régionale des domaines et du cadastre (Regional Directorate of State Domains and of the Land Register)
LA	*lettre d'attribution* (allocation letter)
TF	*titre foncier* (ownership title)

Summary

This work suggests a new approach to studying urban and peri-urban land markets. It draws on a systemic analysis of land delivery channels for housing purposes. It is particularly relevant in situations in which different land tenure systems coexist and procedures to obtain land are extremely complex, as in West African cities. The method is applied in this book to the urban and peri-urban areas of Bamako and to its rural hinterland. It stresses the concept of land delivery channels that, looking at the status of tenure at the time when the land is first placed in circulation for residential use, shows both the process whereby this tenure can be improved and what types of transactions take place on the land markets. We distinguish three land delivery channels: (1) a customary channel, (2) a public and parapublic channel, and (3) a private formal channel. The dynamics within each land delivery channel, together with the interrelationship between these channels, constitute what we call the land delivery system. This approach makes it possible to anticipate the possible consequences for the rest of the system of changes affecting one particular land delivery channel or specific market segment and to get a better grasp of the nature of land conflicts. A better understanding of the land delivery system is undoubtedly a precondition for assessing the likely impact on households of sectoral policy measures concerning access to land.

The study takes a multidisciplinary approach involving economics, sociology, anthropology, geography, and law. It draws on both qualitative and quantitative methods, including a series of interviews with key informants and a wide range of stakeholders involved in the land sector in Bamako and its surrounding areas; a detailed review of the literature on land policies, public allocations of land, customary land transfers, land markets, and land disputes in the area during the past two decades; a survey of land transfers involving plots that have not been built and that took place during the three years preceding the survey in the same areas; and a press review focused on land markets and land disputes.

The analysis shows that households have a strong demand for land for housing, but the vast majority of those households have low income and education levels, little access to information, and few social connections. Supply is inadequate to meet this demand. Land is initially provided through two delivery channels. The first one is the customary channel, which predominates in peri-urban areas where land use is being transformed from agricultural to residential, a transformation now gradually extending to the rural hinterland of Bamako. The second is the public and parapublic delivery channel, which involves the administrative allocation of residential plots to inhabitants and the sale of land to developers. These two channels feed into the formal private channel that delivers serviced plots (those with access to water and electricity) with a *titre foncier* [ownership title] at considerably higher prices. Plots in the various channels may be the subject of successive transactions on land markets, with a degree of formality varying according to tenure, legality, and registration of the transactions. Because the development of the formal market is being severely hindered by a number of factors—complex procedures, very high cost of formalization, and risks of disputes over titles—informal land markets are tolerated, if not encouraged, by the administration. Although informal markets allow low- and middle-income households to gain access to plots, security of tenure is by no means guaranteed, and prices remain high because these informal markets also attract speculators and wealthy and well-connected buyers for whom formalizing tenure is easier. The poorest households have no solution other than rented housing.

Land transfers are characterized by asymmetry in access to information and to administrative and political power. The sustained growth in land prices, high transaction costs, and time-consuming formalization procedures, together with the involvement of a large number of stakeholders and the multiplicity of tenure systems, combine to reduce affordability significantly and make access to secure land very difficult for the urban poor. In the presence of numerous distortions in the allocation of land, land use is bound to be inefficient and access to land particularly inequitable. This inequity is likely to have costly long-term social, economic, and environmental implications that contribute to the uncontrolled spatial expansion of the city with low occupation density and the perpetuation and expansion of informal settlements farther and farther away from the city center with no security of tenure and limited access to services and infrastructure. It also gives rise to many conflicts involving local people, local authorities, the state, the land administration, politicians, and holders of customary rights, especially in the peri-urban areas and rural hinterland of Bamako.

Chapter 1

Introduction

Land Issues in Cities in Sub-Saharan Africa

Unlike other regions in the world, countries in Sub-Saharan Africa share strong similarities in the legal and institutional frameworks that govern their land and land tenure systems and face comparable challenges. Francophone and Lusophone countries in Western and Central Africa[1] have inherited similar civil codes from the colonial era. In addition, state powers in land matters are still governed in most cases by the principle of "presumption of state ownership," whereby any land for which an ownership title has not been issued—or for which a registration procedure in the name of an individual or legal entity is being undertaken—belongs to the state. In these countries, land is still allocated, to a large extent, by the state and, following decentralization measures in an increasing number of countries, by local authorities. Recipients are usually granted personal use rights (evidenced by a temporary permit to develop or occupy the land) or, much more rarely, directly a real right (evidenced by an ownership title). During the past three decades major structural changes in land delivery channels (see chapter 2 for definitions) have occurred with the implementation of legal and economic reforms: the adoption of new land codes that recognize customary forms of tenure, at least in principle; the liberalization of land markets; institutional and political changes, in particular decentralization policies that transfer some land management and administration prerogatives to local entities; and the democratization process.

These changes have occurred in a context of weak governance, insufficient human and financial resources, and limited institutional capacity in the land sector. The converging efforts by aid and development agencies and international finance institutions to accelerate the development of formal private land markets (that is, land markets that operate within legal and regulatory frameworks) have rarely been accompanied by major changes in the way land is accessed. However, compliance with formal sets of rules frequently applies only to some steps but not to others within the same land delivery process. For instance, the allocation of an administrative document is a formal procedure, but the sale of the land to which it applies is prohibited (although very common).

The development of a formal land market[2] has been limited by a series of factors, including land prices that are unaffordable for the vast majority of urban households (who have low and irregular income from informal employment activities), a weak housing finance system, overcomplicated tenure formalization and titling procedures, widespread corruption in land administration, and weak land registration and information systems. Conversely, informal markets, which are considerably more accessible to lower- and middle-income groups, have grown sharply.

Land markets in Sub-Saharan African cities are characterized by heavy pressure on land in urban and peri-urban areas extending up to the rural hinterland of cities (see table 2.1). This increasing demand for land[3] comes up against limited supply in the formal private land delivery channels or through public land delivery channels (chapters 2 and 3). As a matter of fact, access to land for housing is still marked by a range of tenure arrangements and a tendency to use the less expensive customary land delivery channel and informal markets (chapters 3 and 4). Between 60 percent and 80 percent of the urban population in Sub-Saharan African cities is estimated to live in informal settlements (UN-Habitat 2010). As a result, most cities are characterized by the coexistence of various land delivery channels with different levels of formality, legality, and legitimacy. A series of obstacles hinders most efforts to reform land administration institutions. Conventional policy options, tools, and procedures tentatively implemented during the past few decades to streamline and unify land markets and improve land administration have achieved limited results (Rochegude and Plançon 2010).

The Example of Bamako, Mali

Understanding Land Delivery Channels for Housing and Land Markets

Given its history and prevailing tenure system; legal, regulatory, and institutional framework; administrative practices and recent attempts to improve land management; spatial patterns; rate of urbanization; and social organization, Bamako is to a large extent representative of the prevailing situation in Western African cities (UN-Habitat 2010). Attempting to improve the understanding of the drivers and complexities of land delivery channels and land markets in Bamako, as well as their determining factors, reveals the challenges that have hindered the implementation of urban projects in Mali.[4] The land delivery issue is also important for Mali inasmuch as unequal access to land, the very large proportion of tenants who are among the most disadvantaged, and of people accommodated free of charge in Bamako District (43.4 percent and 10.2 percent, respectively, according to the 2009 census [INSTAT 2011]), and the weaknesses of land governance have greatly contributed to social unrest and instability (see chapter 4). A march of "land victims" saw more than 2,000 protesters in Bamako on March 12, 2012, about a week before the coup that resulted in the ousting of President Amadou Toumani Touré.[5] In early April 2014, a sit-in was organized for several days at the Bamako labor exchange by cooperatives and associations of victims of expropriation who were received by the prime minister.[6] In spite of increased awareness of the political risks of mismanagement in land administration and of tenure insecurity harming many households,[7] the effective implementation of more transparent modes of land access is severely impeded by clientelistic practices and the weak economic environment, in particular the limited opportunities for wealth creation that make investing in land one of the only options.

Better understanding of current metropolitan area–wide land and housing practices, of the functioning of land markets, and of the formation of land prices is a precondition for designing any sustainable land and housing policy. For these reasons, identifying the options available to the different income and social groups for access to land, tenure, and location is important. These options are determined by affordability as well as by access to information, ability to interact with the land administration, and participation in clientelistic relationships. Attempts to formalize land markets through, among others, the creation of a parastatal land development agency in 1992, the Agence de cession immobilière (ACI), have introduced formal land market mechanisms into a land delivery system (see definition in chapter 2) dominated by informal and customary practices and, at the central and local government levels, a land administration undermined by corruption, clientelism, and political interference—land is frequently allotted at preferential prices on the basis of political affiliation (Bertrand 1998).[8] Safeguard measures—such as the program Sauvons notre Quartier (Save Our Neighborhood), which was implemented in Bamako between 1993 and 1996 to mitigate the social impact of market pressure on the urban poor—that intended to combine physical upgrading in informal settlements and the resettlement of displaced households were diverted from and did not achieve their objectives.[9] Many regularization operations have been launched by the *communes* (administrative jurisdictions headed by a mayor) without having first obtained an allocation from the state's private domain, while land and property development companies are playing a considerably greater role in the land markets. It is thus fair to say that, during the past few decades, land markets have been left in the hands of stakeholders and institutions that operated autonomously without transparent procedures and without government guidance or strategic guidelines.

Demographic Pressure, Urbanization, and Demand for Land for Housing

Mali is a country of 14.5 million inhabitants. About one-third of the population was urbanized as of 2010. The Bamako urban area (Bamako District and a large part of the eight adjoining rural communes[10]) has been absorbing a very large share of the rural-to-urban migration, which typically follows the path described in Box 1.1 and, adding to already high natural population growth, results in strong demographic pressure and a young population.

On the basis of the 2009 population census projections and plausible assumptions regarding the urbanization rate in the peripheral communes (INSTAT 2011), it can be estimated that about 2,350,000 people were living in the urban area of Bamako in 2011, of which 1,987,000 (85 percent) were living in the core district.[11] Figures from the 1998 and 2009 censuses indicate that the population in Bamako District has increased by 4.8 percent annually, while the annual growth rate of the population in the eight communes has been even higher, ranging from 6.2 percent to 17.2 percent. If the overall annual population growth rate during the next 20 years remains in the range of 4.5 percent (a conservative estimate), the population of the city would reach 3.5 million in 2020 and about 5 million in 2030.[12] On this basis, assuming that average household

BOX 1.1

A Migrant's Demand for Land

In Ville de Bamako (2012, p. 132), Hamidou Magassa describes the journey of a young man coming to Bamako from the countryside: "To become a proper *Bamakois* [resident of Bamako], someone heading to the city from the countryside has a long way to go across the whole gamut of urban and peri-urban tenure arrangements before finally settling. As a young unmarried migrant with few resources, he will be taken in by a landlord, usually a relative or an acquaintance from the village, who has come to the city before him. After a few months or years of informal activity and with permission from his landlord, whose family may still provide him with meals, this long-term migrant will not leave the neighborhood but move towards renting a room, either shared or otherwise. Having mastered a craft and achieved professional stability with a regular income, he will take a wife and gain his conjugal independence, in terms of both board and lodging, by renting two or three rooms in a family compound, with some degree of linkage to the original landlord. To escape the uncontrollable pressure of monthly renting in Bamako, acquiring a residential plot will become his prime objective that he will achieve either officially (via the administration) or informally (customary system) in the peri-urban area. Building and setting up as a property owner will take this now fifty-something head of a polygamous household quite a few years before he, in his turn, takes charge of around 20 people." (translation from the original by the authors) size and land consumption remain unchanged, an additional 5,200 hectares of urban land will be required by 2020 and nearly 12,000 hectares by 2030 to cope with the demand for residential land.[13] These projections would thus require a sharp increase in the provision of land for housing.

Economic, Financial, and Political Changes Stimulating the Demand for Land

The demand for land for housing has increased as a response to the steady increase, until recently, in the incomes of urban households;[14] the emergence of an urban middle class that nevertheless remains fairly small;[15] massive remittances from Malian expatriates, of which part is invested in land; and changes in urban family structures and norms.[16]

Other financial and economic factors have also played a role in stimulating the demand for land: because of weak savings institutions and the scarcity of opportunities for investment, and in a context of limited social protection, holders of monetary assets or idle funds view land as a profitable and inflation-proof investment. With the development of the market economy, land can also be seen as an asset that could allow access to mortgage finance. Nevertheless, although provision of land by ACI during the past two decades and demand for land from formal private developers have contributed to the development of housing finance institutions, the lending system in Mali remains limited to short-term credit. The lending system is also hampered by weak public administration capacity; a poor vital records system, in particular faulty identity and birth certificates; and lack of reliability of the *titre foncier* [ownership title] used as collateral.

Speculative investments also add significantly to the demand for land.[17] Land market activity in Bamako is partly driven by speculative strategies as many investors look for land to buy, expecting a price increase with the future incorporation of the land into the urbanized area or following improvement of the tenure status of the land. Speculative investments in the rural hinterland have been observed as far as 70–80 kilometers away from the city center. According to agents and brokers, this speculation is sustained by investments from Bamako-based merchants and from expatriate Malian communities. Speculative strategies are also encouraged by widespread illicit practices and corruption among government institutions and local administrations (chapter 4).

Insecurity in the North facilitates illegal trading activities that generate income, which can get recycled through the land market, contributing to additional speculation. According to the Groupe intergouvernemental d'action contre le blanchiment d'argent en Afrique de l'Ouest (GIABA), 2010 (p. 31), "Weak regulation of real estate combined with the traditional land tenure system makes it difficult to prevent criminals from purchasing properties with the proceeds from illegal activities." (translation by the authors)

Increases in Land Prices in Urban and Peri-Urban Areas

Especially since 2007, land prices have steadily increased in Bamako's urban and peri-urban areas (with several observers mentioning annual increases of up to 100 percent in some locations), further stimulating the demand for land in expectation of further increases. The disappearance of cheap options for accessing land may have been exacerbated by the upgrade from affordable to more expensive land tenure forms (for those who can afford it or who benefit from good personal links with the land administration).

The Relationship between Land Delivery and Political Cycles

Political cycles (elections) in Bamako exhibit some parallels with allocation of land plots by the state or local authorities and with the real estate business cycle: before elections, allocation of land plots may serve a political clientele. After elections, candidates who have gone into debt to finance their campaigns may be tempted to pay off their debts by selling in their own name plots obtained from the state to develop housing. This observation is corroborated by key informants involved in land allocations and transactions as well as by the work of researchers (Bertrand 2006; Coulibaly and Touré 2009).[18]

Purpose of the Study, Positioning in Relation to Existing Literature, and Organization of the Work

The purpose and originality of this study lie in considering that land markets operate within delivery channels for residential land (see definitions in chapter 2). The starting premise is that the plots and land intended for housing that are the subject of land-market transactions have a history starting with their first use as predominantly residential land and continuing over time, with possible changes in the status of tenure and type of holder.[19] These are the changes, described as accurately as possible and in relation to each of the land delivery channels, that help show how closely and in what way formal and informal land markets are interlinked and that a political decision concerning land, with scope that seems limited at first glance, can affect all delivery channels and markets. The analysis highlights these links and interdependencies in the delivery system for residential land, and underscores the diversity of stakeholders and institutions involved in land markets, the gaps between actual practice and rules established by the state, and the causes of many land disputes and conflicts. The concept of a land delivery system also helps provide a better grasp of the mechanisms whereby urban expansion gradually encroaches on agricultural land and stresses the consequences of this process for changes in land tenure and price. Consequently, the analysis takes a particular interest in the peri-urban areas of Bamako and its rural hinterland, where there have been many changes in land use. The study relies on contributions from several disciplines—anthropology, economics, sociology, law, and geography—and on an approach with both qualitative and quantitative aspects.

It must be pointed out that the study does not deal with property markets (acquisition and rental of housing) nor with the rental market for plots of land. These undoubtedly have an influence on nonrental land markets (purchase and sale). There are also many tenants and people accommodated free of charge who aspire to have land on which to build a house. In addition, a number of households buy land with the aim of renting out some of it or renting out one or several rooms once the house has been built. An analysis of the interactions between land markets (purchase and sale), the plot rental market, and property markets would require additional research with particular emphasis on household surveys that could not be undertaken as part of this study that focuses on the single and already complex issue of access to land.

This study is a continuation of work relating to modes of access to land and urban land markets in Sub-Saharan Africa. Other authors who have looked at this issue—including with regard to Bamako—have nevertheless not stressed the links between the different channels.

Concerning Sub-Saharan Africa, Rakodi and Leduka (2004) propose a seven-category classification of modes of access to land based on studies undertaken in a sample of cities.[20] The authors suggest that cases of squatting *sensu stricto* are uncommon. In their view, informal modes of access to land are to some extent a continuation of land administration practices that took account of customary tenure systems, regardless of whether recognized or codified by colonial and postcolonial governments. The social legitimacy of the social groups holding customary rights over land—initially rural but destined to become urban—has been maintained, and that organizational capacity enables those groups to impose their institutions on their members and many of the people who purchase their land.

Drawing on the examples of Addis Ababa, Accra, Dakar, and Johannesburg, Wehrmann (2008) presents five channels, grouping together some of the categories suggested by the previous authors and establishing a distinction, which is not always easy to do, between customary and neocustomary systems on the one hand and between legal, illegal, extralegal, and criminal operations on the other. In the two studies referred to here, the authors include land markets in land delivery channels, but consider that transfers on customary land take place outside the market.

By looking at both the production of land and modes of access, Durand-Lasserve (2004) identifies three typical land and property production channels[21] based on two essential criteria: the different phases in the process of land production and the public and private stakeholders involved. He stresses the links between channels and introduces the notion of a system: "at the scale of a city, we can therefore speak of a system of land and property production, with any change affecting one channel having repercussions on the operation of all the others" (translation from the original by the authors) (Durand-Lasserve 2004, p. 1189).

There have been many studies of urban land markets in Sub-Saharan Africa. This analysis draws primarily on works that refer to the links between the different markets and on works that explain the development of informal markets in light of the fact that great poverty and complex, lengthy, and costly procedures for accessing land and improving the status of tenure within the law coexist with very high land prices on formal markets (Antwi 2000; Leduka 2004; Kironde 2004; Marx 2007; UN-Habitat 2010; Napier 2010; Syagga 2010).

Various studies have been conducted with regard to Malian cities and Bamako and its periphery in particular, each of them dealing with a specific aspect of the system.

Bertrand (2006), for example, demonstrates the cyclical changes undergone by land management in Bamako District. She had previously presented the "three land regimes" of the capital city and compared the public supply of plots with household demand, stressing the segmentation of land supply and the impossibility of speaking of a land market that would not be subject to social and political pressure (Bertrand 1995, 1998). Bourdarias (1999, 2006) exposes the conflicts around the occupation and holding of plots in a neighborhood of Bamako commune I and that neighborhood's expansion into a rural village, going on to analyze the use of tradition that the various groups of stakeholders in conflict interpret in different ways.

Regarding Kati *cercle* (an administrative jurisdiction that includes several communes), adjacent to Bamako, Djiré (2006) highlights the rapid increase in the number of ownership titles issued as of the mid-1990s for the benefit of the urban elite and to the detriment of farmers. He describes the procedures required to obtain such titles and their costs (Djiré 2007). With other authors, he suggests solutions to provide legal security for land transactions (Djiré and Traore 2008) and analyzes the monetized transactions involving agricultural land at five sites, including two in Kati cercle (Keita and Djiré 2009). Farvacque-Vitkovic and others (2007), in the part of their study concerning land, attribute the exacerbation of difficulties for the majority of the urban population of Mali, and Bamako in particular, to the very high costs and centralization of the procedures required to obtain an ownership title, together with the exhaustion of the state's land reserves, given that land management is marked by clientelism.

Durand-Lasserve (2009) looks more specifically, in a commune in that same cercle, at the way prices rise as tenure status becomes more secure. Bouju and others (2009) study the social and cultural aspects of land transactions on several sites, including two in Bamako District and two more in Kati cercle. Again in that cercle, but some distance from Bamako, in Soro village, Baguineda commune, Becker (2013) studies the consequences for village social life of the emergence of land markets and the move from customary land ownership to private ownership.

Chapter 2 presents the method adopted for the study. Chapter 3 describes the different land delivery channels, and chapter 4 explains the links between the different channels making up the land delivery system and describes the conflicts that run through the system. Chapter 5 presents the results of a survey of land plots prepared on the basis of the lessons learned from the analysis of the land delivery system.[22] Because the focus is on land plots that where the subject of transfers within the three years before the survey, the chapter provides information on the transactions carried out on the land markets during a short period.

Notes

1. West Africa includes 8 French-speaking countries out of 15 and Central Africa 7 French-speaking countries out of 10. Mali is a part of Francophone West Africa.
2. For a definition of formal and informal markets, see chapter 2.
3. Sub-Saharan Africa had 863 million inhabitants in 2010, of whom 37 percent were urban dwellers. In 2025, the population is projected to reach 1.2 billion, 45 percent of whom will live in cities. The urban population is thus expected to increase by 220 million between 2010 and 2025 (UN-Habitat 2010).
4. See in particular the serious implementation challenges faced by the World Bank–funded Third Urban Project (1996–2005) presented in Farvacque-Vitkovic and others (2007).
5. "Litiges fonciers: Plus de deux mille personnes ont marché ce mardi pour réclamer justice," *Afribone Mali*, March 13, 2012.
6. "Sit-In des victimes d'expropriation : haute tension à la Bourse du travail," *L'Indicateur du Renouveau*, April 3, 2014.
7. A series of measures was announced in 2014 by the government of Mali to reform land administration: a land information system will be progressively set up; the transfer of State Domains land to individuals and companies is suspended for a renewable period of 6 months; and the Directorate of State Domains and Land Register in the District of Bamako and the Kati Circle will be audited and their archives secured (Source: "Le ministre des Domaines de l'Etat, Tieman Coulibaly, hier face à la presse," *L'Indépendant*, September 5, 2014). An active fight against corruption in the land sector has been launched to curb fraud and related land speculation.
8. This has been repeatedly corroborated in the course of this study by observations and interviews with key informants among a wide range of stakeholders involved in land administration and land markets.
9. Farvacque-Vitkovic and others (2007, p. 20) describe the situation as follows: "In 1992, the District of Bamako undertook a program called *Sauvons notre quartier*

(SNQ - Save Our Neighborhood) with the aim of rapidly restructuring 24 informal settlements in Bamako. Various political, institutional, financial, land ownership and operational issues revealed the shortcomings of the program intended to improve living conditions for the poor. SNQ never managed to assert real control over the land in either the informal settlements or the planned resettlement areas. The resettlement areas were systematically occupied by new squatters, instead of the people they were originally intended for. Progressively, all control of land management was lost and Mali's government had to suspend the allocation of plots for the first time in 1996 in order to halt land speculation. This effectively ended the SNQ initiative." (Translation from the original by the authors.)

10. Communes of Baguineda-Camp, Dialakorodji, Dogodouman, Kalabancoro, Mandé, Moribabougou, Mountougoula, and N'Gabacoro in Kati cercle.

11. There is an ongoing debate concerning the creation of Greater Bamako, which would attach some of the peri-urban communes to the current district (Ville de Bamako 2012).

12. According to the report "Bamako 2030" (Ville de Bamako 2012), which assumes an annual population growth rate for the district of 5.4 percent, the population of Bamako District alone is predicted to reach 6 million by 2030.

13. This crude estimate of the long-term requirement for land for housing is indicative. It only covers the need for residential plots and excludes land requirements for primary infrastructure. It does not take account of the likely lower incomes of internal migrant households, and thus of their smaller land consumption (although this may vary with the type of tenure and location and thus with corresponding land prices). The estimate does not take account of other parameters likely to result in a densification of the city, such as the expected demographic transition (especially in cities), the likely decline in household size for economic and cultural reasons, or possible changes in the physical patterns of human settlement (with the development of condominium multistory housing units and other types of housing that allow higher urban population density). Nor does it consider the impact of regularization policies or the renewal and redevelopment of city center settlements, which are likely to increase population density but will be accompanied by increased demand for land for resettlement in the periphery of Bamako.

14. However, the real GDP growth rate slowed sharply in 2011 (to 2.7 percent), resulting in a 0.3 percent drop in real GDP per capita (African Development Bank and others 2012). According to *Perspectives économiques en Afrique*, August, 25, 2014, the real GDP per capita growth was negative in 2012 (−4.2 percent). In 2013, it was estimated at + 2 percent.

15. According to African Development Bank (2011), the middle class, characterized by a per capita daily consumption of $4–$20 per day, represents only 8.1 percent of the population of Mali.

16. Although there is no certainty that changes in family structure and norms have contributed to a change in the demand for land, it is not unlikely that the effect of a modestly decreasing fertility rate in urban areas will have been more than offset by children moving out of their parents' dwellings, thus increasing the demand for land.

17. Speculative investments are those that are not intended to develop the purchased land or to make productive use of it, but to keep it undeveloped and put it back onto the market when the value has increased.

18. On this topic, Coulibaly and Traoré (in Ville de Bamako 2012, p. 99) report an interview with the director of a project engineering and territorial development consultancy who declares, "The political system is somewhat perverse in Mali, inasmuch as anyone wishing to be elected first on the list will have to fund the bulk of the campaign. This means that some people will get into debt to do so, telling themselves that they can recoup their outlay after the elections by selling or subdividing some land." (translation from the original by the authors).

19. Inheritances form part of the history of land and plots. If the heirs keep the plot, have the transfer registered (which is relatively uncommon), and do not change the status of its tenure, the plot's history provisionally stops there.

20. Eldoret, Kenya; Enugu, Nigeria; Gaborone, Botswana; Kampala, Uganda; Lusaka, Zambia; and Maseru, Lesotho. The seven categories are (1) allocation of public land, (2) purchase of land through the market, (3) delivery of customary land through state-sanctioned channels, (4) delivery of land through customary channels to members of the group, (5) purchase of customary land, (6) allocation by officials, and (7) self allocation. The categories may be larger or smaller depending on the city concerned, and it is often difficult to make a clear distinction between them.

21. State, capitalist, and popular channels.

22. The survey, conducted between February and April 2012, covers Bamako District and Bamako's peri-urban areas and rural hinterland.

References

African Development Bank. 2011. "The Middle of the Pyramid: Dynamics of the Middle Class in Africa." *Market brief*, April 20.

———, Organisation for Economic Co-operation and Development, United Nations Development Programme, and United Nations Economic Commission for Africa. 2012. *African Economic Outlook 2012.* Paris: OECD Publishing.

Antwi, A. 2000. "Urban Land Markets in Sub-Saharan Africa: A Quantitative Study of Accra, Ghana." Dissertation, Napier University, Edinburgh, Scotland.

Becker, L. 2013. "Land Sales and the Transformation of Social Relations and Landscape in Peri-Urban Mali." *Geoforum* 46: 113–23.

Bertrand, M. 1995. "Bamako, d'une République à l'autre." *Annales de la Recherche Urbaine* 66: 40–51.

———. 1998. "Marchés fonciers en transition: le cas de Bamako, Mali." *Annales de Géographie* 602: 381–409.

———. 2006. "Foncier débridé/foncier bridé: enjeu récent de la décentralisation ou alternance centrale dans l'histoire longue des communes urbaines maliennes." In *Décentralisation des pouvoirs en Afrique en contrepoint des modèles territoriaux français*, edited by Claude Fay, 179–98. Paris: Institut de Recherche pour le Développement.

Bouju, J., A. Ausseil, M. F. Ba, M. Ballo, H. Bocoum, and C. Touquent. 2009. "Dynamique des transactions foncières au Mali: Mountougoula, Baguinéda, centre ville de Bamako, Bandagiara et Ningari." IRAM/CEAMA, Paris and Aix-en-Provence.

Bourdarias, F. 1999. "La ville mange la terre: désordres fonciers aux confins de Bamako." *Journal des Anthropologues* 77–78: 141–60.

———. 2006. "La décentralisation, la coutume et la loi: les constructions imaginaires d'un conflit à la périphérie de Bamako (Mali)." In *Décentralisation des pouvoirs en Afrique en contrepoint des modèles territoriaux français*, edited by Claude Fay, 221–38. Paris: Institut de Recherche pour le Développement.

Coulibaly, J., and M. Touré. 2009. "Étude sur les pratiques de gouvernance urbaine." Étude de cas – Mali, technical report. Institut des Sciences et des Techniques de l'Equipement et de l'Environnement pour le Développement.

Djiré, M. 2006. "Immatriculation et appropriation foncière dans une zone péri-urbaine du Mali - Les avatars d'une procédure (nécessaire ?)." Paper prepared for the symposium "Les frontières de la question foncière / At the frontiers of land issues," Montpellier, France, May 17–19.

———. 2007. "Les paysans maliens exclus de la propriété foncière? Les avatars de l'appropriation par le titre foncier." Dossier No. 144, International Institute for Environment and Development, London.

———, and K. Traoré. 2008. "Assurer la sécurisation légale des transactions foncières: quel rôle pour les intermédiaires et facilitateurs?" Études de cas en zone péri-urbaine et dans le Mali-Sud, Support to the Legal Empowerment of the Poor, Legal Empowerment in Practice – LEP Working Paper, Food and Agriculture Organization of the United Nations.

Durand-Lasserve, A. 2004. "La question foncière dans les villes du Tiers Monde: un bilan." *Economies et Sociétés* 38 (7): 1183–211.

———. 2009. "Harmonisation des systèmes fonciers au Mali par une intégration du droit coutumier au droit formel." Programme d'appui aux collectivités territoriales (Division Gestion du foncier communal), GTZ, Mali.

Farvacque-Vitkovic, C., A. Casalis, M. Diop, and C. Eghoff. 2007. "Development of the Cities of Mali: Challenges and Priorities." Africa Region Working Paper 104a, World Bank, Washington, DC.

Groupe intergouvernemental d'action contre le blanchiment d'argent en Afrique de l'Ouest (GIABA). 2010. "Rapport de typologies : blanchiment des produits du trafic de stupéfiants en Afrique de l'Ouest." December. Dakar.

INSTAT (Institut National de la Statistique). 2011. "4ème Recensement Général de la population et de l'habitat du Mali (RGPH)." Résultats définitifs, Novembre.

Keita, A., and M. Djiré. 2009. "Les transactions foncières en zones rurales et périurbaines du Mali: quelles leçons pour la loi sur le foncier agricole?" Working paper, Groupe d'étude et de recherche Sociologie et droit appliqué, Faculté des Sciences Juridiques et Politiques de l'Université de Bamako.

Kironde, J. M. L. 2004. "Current Changes in Customary/Traditional Land Delivery Systems in Sub-Saharan African Cities: The Case of Dar es Salaam." University College of Lands and Architectural Studies, Dar-es-Salaam.

Leduka, C. R. 2004. "Informal Land Delivery Processes in Mazeru, Lesotho. Summary of Findings and Policy Implications." Policy Brief No. 4, International Development Department, School of Public Policy, University of Birmingham.

Marx, C. 2007. *Do Informal Land Markets Work for Poor People? An Assessment of Three Metropolitan Cities in South Africa.* Synthesis report, Isandla Institute and Stephen Berrisford Consulting, with Progressus Research and Development, Urban LandMark, Kenilworth, South Africa.

Napier, M. 2010. *Urban Land Markets: Economic Concepts and Tools for Engaging in Africa, Handbook for Practitioners.* Nairobi, Kenya: UN-Habitat.

Rakodi, C., and C. Leduka. 2004. "Informal Land Delivery Process and Access to Land for the Poor: A Comparative Study of Six African Cities." Policy Brief 6, University of Birmingham, Birmingham, U.K.

Rochegude, A., and C. Plançon. 2010. *Décentralisation, acteurs locaux et foncier: fiches pays.* Agence Française de Développement et Ministère des Affaires Etrangères et Européennes, Paris, France.

Syagga, P. 2010. "A Study of the East African Urban Land Market." FinMark Trust and UN-Habitat, Nairobi, Kenya.

UN-Habitat. 2010. *The State of African Cities 2010. Governance, Inequality and Urban Land Markets.* Nairobi, Kenya: United Nations.

Ville de Bamako. 2012. *Bamako 2030: croissance et développement - Imaginer des stratégies urbaines pour un avenir maîtrisé et partagé.*

Wehrmann, B. 2008. "Dynamics of Peri-Urban Land Markets in Sub-Saharan Africa: Adherence to the Virtue of Common Property vs. Quest for Individual Gain." *Erkunde* 62 (1): 75–88.

Chapter 2

Methodology of the Study

A Systemic Approach to Land Delivery Channels and Land Markets

To better understand the nature of transactions involving land, it is important to position such transactions within the process that led to the land being put up for sale. This process can be placed within one of the land delivery channels, but those channels are not completely separate. Because of the many links between them, this analysis speaks of a land delivery system that includes formal and informal land markets. Any change affecting one component within one land delivery channel has impacts on other channels and consequently on the whole land delivery system. For instance, a land price increase in a given delivery channel will drive households toward other delivery channels (via a substitution effect). The systemic approach to land delivery channels and markets used in this book gives a better idea of the nature of the social conflicts that often arise at the point at which the different channels intersect and is particularly relevant to the study of cities characterized by rapid expansion and multiple forms of land tenure.

Land delivery channels encompass all the stages in the process through which land (1) is characterized by a particular tenure status when first sold or allocated as essentially residential land; (2) can be the subject of improvement in that status, on a gradual basis and sometimes to the extent of obtaining a *titre foncier* [ownership title] (complete tenure formalization), which is rarely achieved by the first buyers or those to whom land was allotted; and (3) is sold on land markets before or after tenure formalization. The concept of a land delivery channel complements that of a land market, which refers only to land transactions at a given time, irrespective of the initial tenure status or stage of the formalization process at which the transaction takes place.[1] Knowing not only the initial tenure status and possibilities of improvement but also the different markets on which that land can be sold helps provide an understanding of the interrelations between the different land delivery channels. These interrelations justify the use of the phrase "land delivery system," which includes the three channels identified in the present study and their interrelations. Identifying initial tenure status is particularly important in peri-urban areas and in the rural hinterland because it makes it possible to understand, for instance, how agricultural land is incrementally being transformed into urban land and thus situates land markets in a historical and dynamic perspective. A residential plot supplied on the market often has a customary and agricultural origin, which means that any change in the supply of customary land may have an impact on the land market segments on which it can be sold. Valuable indications of the degree of tenure security to which those acquiring plots can aspire can be gained from knowing the stages in the long and costly formalization process whereby the tenure status of the land or plot can be improved, and from knowing whether the rules relating to transactions have been observed. Lessons learned from the analysis make it easier to understand differences between formal and informal markets (as defined later in this section) and the diversity of land market segments with regard to tenure type, compliance with the rules relating to land transactions, and accessibility for households in view of their resources and social networks.

Each type of land delivery channel is characterized by (1) the tenure status of the land the first time it is sold or allocated for residential use; (2) the channel's organization and the steps to be taken to improve the status of the land and succeed in formalizing tenure; (3) the parties involved; and (4) land values (whether market or nonmarket based).

In this study, particular attention is given to (1) the relation between land allocation by public authorities and market transactions, and between formal and informal land markets; (2) the diversity of tenure options on the different land delivery channels; (3) the consequences that the different types of tenure can have for tenure security and land values; and (4) the interrelations between the land delivery channels within the land delivery system. Whereas the vast majority of studies tend to focus on one particular land delivery channel or land market segment, very few (such as Bertrand 1998) have established and studied the relationships between the different elements of the system.

The formal and informal markets are so interconnected that establishing a clear distinction between them can be difficult. It is preferable to note that there are degrees of formality of markets according to three criteria: (1) the type of document acknowledging the transaction and its registration (see annex 4A); (2) recognition that the seller possesses the document or title relating to tenure (see table 3.1); and (3) whether the rules established by the state have been observed. The most formal market, where all the rules established by the state are observed, involves transactions on plots with ownership titles or precarious titles authenticated in notarial deeds. The most informal market is the market on which transactions in customary land take place with simple, nonauthenticated certificates of sale (for a graphical representation of these markets, see figure 4.2).

Along with that of other researchers, the analysis here suggests that informal land markets are not anarchic. Syagga (2010, p. 4) notes the importance of informal markets for the majority of inhabitants of East Africa and insists that informality does not mean that there are no rules: "in all cases—however informal the system may appear in legal terms—the land transaction processes are structured, guided by communal norms and procedures, and play a major role in overcoming the delivery failure of formal urban land markets."

Combining Qualitative and Quantitative Approaches

First, we documented the functioning of the land delivery system. This was done, qualitatively, through (1) an assessment of the legal and institutional framework governing land administration and management in Bamako and surrounding areas; (2) meetings with key stakeholders involved in land delivery;[2] and (3) identification of the way land is transferred, possible changes in tenure status, and the role of stakeholders involved in these operations. Particular attention was given to factual information provided by press articles, especially during the past three years (2012–2014). This was complemented, quantitatively, with a survey of recent land transfers carried out throughout Bamako and its peri-urban areas and rural hinterland.

It should be noted that the study was carried out in a particular administrative, socioeconomic, and political context characterized by (1) the suspension of state allocations of land in the state's private domain to *communes* (administrative jurisdictions headed by a mayor) and developers; (2) the suspension of allocation of *concessions rurales*[3] and their conversion into ownership titles; (3) legal changes in the judicial procedures in cases of conflict about ownership of land with ownership titles; (4) rising population concerns and social unrest about mismanagement and corruption in land administration; and (5) political change and instability following the March 22, 2012, coup and the military defeat of government forces in the northern provinces.

This study should not lead the reader to believe that the observed land dynamics are irreversible. The measures taken by the government of Mali since the second half of 2014 could lead to a significant reform of the land sector (see chapter 1).

Study Area

The study focused on residential land, with emphasis on the transformation of rural (mainly agricultural) land into urban (mainly residential) land. For this reason, the study area extends far beyond the urbanized areas of Bamako (continuous and high-density developments) and its peri-urban areas (mixed rural and residential land use) in continuity with the existing urban fabric. The study also covers the rural hinterland of Bamako, which includes parts of the territory of all adjoining communes in Kati *cercle* (administrative jurisdiction that includes several communes), and some parts of communes in the Koulikoro cercle adjoining Kati cercle (map 2.1).[4]

Although these different zones are not officially defined, the urban and peri-urban areas can be distinguished by field observation and satellite imagery. The urban area is characterized by built up contiguity; the peri-urban area by a mix of rural areas, incorporating core villages and both agricultural and uncultivated land that is being subdivided, built up, and integrated into

Map 2.1 Study Area

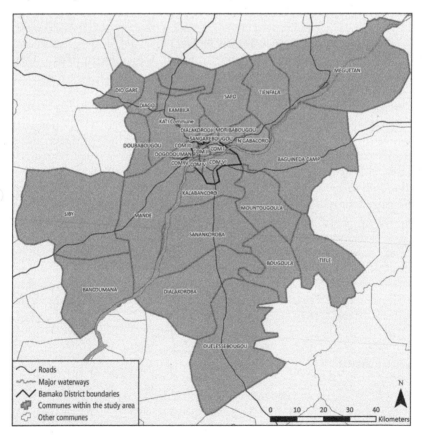

Source: Map prepared by Brian Blankespoor using data from Direction Nationale des Collectivités Territoriales.

Table 2.1 Characteristics of Urban and Peri-Urban Areas and of the Rural Hinterland

Areas	Built-up area and population density	Physical characteristics	Land market patterns and prices
Urban areas	Built up contiguity	Dense road and infrastructure network	Fully monetized land markets
	High and high to medium density		High and medium land prices
Peri-urban areas	Land subdivision and development in progress	Road and infrastructure network under construction	Usually fully monetized land markets
	Medium and low density		Medium and low land prices
Rural hinterland of Bamako	Low density, except in core villages or along main roads	Predominantly agricultural use	Coexistence of monetized and custom-based transfers
		Formation of agricultural estates	Low land prices (but higher than outside the zone of influence of the urban area)

the urban area, and buildings being erected at low density. The rural hinterland does not have visible physical characteristics enabling it to be identified through satellite imagery. It can be defined as the rural area that is under the direct land market influence of the city, mainly reflected in land prices, which are higher than land prices in other rural areas that have similar physical characteristics and agricultural potential (see table 2.1). Consequently, the rural hinterland to be covered by the survey could not be identified before the field work but only in the course of the study, on the basis of recorded land transactions and land prices.[5]

Notes

1. See Dowall (1995) for a description of the standard tool for land market assessments in developing countries.
2. The authors met with village headmen, village councilors, and inhabitants in nine villages in seven communes (Sanankoroba village in Sanankoroba commune, Kanadjiguila village in Mandé commune, Dialakoroba village in Dialakoroba commune, Kabala and Niamana villages in Kalabancoro commune, Marako and Banankoro villages in Ouelessebougou commune, Kakabougou village in Baguineda-Camp commune, and Faraba village in Faraba commune); mayors and deputies in three communes in Kati cercle; a mayor of one commune in Bamako; a deputy mayor of Bamako District; the governor and his chief of staff at Bamako District; officials of DNDC (Direction nationale des domaines et du cadastre), DRDC (Direction régionale des domaines et du cadastre), and DDB-DC (Direction des domaines et du cadastre du District de Bamako); the heads of the Urban Planners Association of Mali (Ordre des urbanistes du Mali), Property Developers Association of Mali (Association des promoteurs immobiliers du Mali), and Rural Engineering

Department (Genie rural); a notary; three coxers (informal brokers); and staff at the World Bank's Bamako office.

3. The Council of Ministers of June 15, 2011, decided to suspend the allocations of CRs.

4. The study covers the communes of Baguineda-Camp, Bancoumana, Bougoula, Diago, Dialakoroba, Dialakorodji, Dio-Gare, Doubabougou, Kalabancoro, Kambila, Kati commune, Mandé, Moribabougou, Mountougoula, N Gabacoro, Ouelessebougou, Safo, Sanankoroba, Sangarebougou, Siby, Tiele in Kati cercle; communes of Meguetan and Tienfala in the Koulikoro cercle; and four communes of Bamako (I, IV, V, and VI).

5. Map 2.1 does not show a boundary between the peri-urban area and the rural hinterland, which would require further work involving processing of satellite imagery.

References

Bertrand, M. 1998. "Marchés fonciers en transition: le cas de Bamako, Mali." *Annales de Géographie* 602: 381–409, Paris.

Dowall, D. 1995. *The Land Market Assessment: A New Tool for Urban Management.* World Bank: Washington, DC.

Syagga, P. 2010. "A Study of the East African Urban Land Market." FinMark Trust and UN-Habitat, Nairobi, Kenya.

Chapter 3

Land Delivery Channels

Three land delivery channels were identified:

- The customary channel, through which the first sales and transfers involve customary land
- The public channel, through which allocations, sales of land, and tenure regularization operations are initially made by public and parapublic authorities
- The formal private channel, through which land and serviced plots (with access to water and electricity) with *titre foncier* [ownership title] are initially sold with notarial deeds or equivalent documentation by property development companies, purchasing cooperatives, or individuals.

As in other cities in the subregion, nonmarket forms of allocation by the state and by local authorities coexist with land markets.

This classification requires the following comments:

First, land markets operate within and across land delivery channels (see figures 3.1, 3.2, 3.3, 4.1, and 4.2).

Second, both legal and nonlegal practices (the latter being greeted with a degree of tolerance or resignation) are found in both land allocations and land market transactions. In the public channel, the procedures established by law and decree regarding allocations, and regularization operations are not always followed, and beneficiaries often do not take the necessary steps to obtain a use or ownership right (precarious title or ownership title). Transactions involving land obtained by private individuals or small property developers from the customary and public channels are usually carried out in the informal sector of the land markets (see figure 4.2).

Third, a variety of tenure situations can be encountered in the different land delivery channels, depending on documentation and conferred rights. Table 3.1 shows the three major categories of documents relating to land tenure. The "administrative document" category refers to documents that are not considered titles, although they are issued by public authorities (state representatives or *communes*, which are administrative jurisdictions headed by a mayor). Precarious titles give their holders rights of use but not ownership.

Table 3.1 Administrative Documents and Titles Associated with Land Tenure

Documents or titles involving representatives of the state or communes and DRDC[a]	Characteristics
ADMINISTRATIVE DOCUMENTS (residential land)	**THESE DOCUMENTS ARE NOT TITLES**
Bulletin or *lettre de convocation* (issued by prefects or subprefects)	Gives evidence of the allocation of a plot following subdivision of farmland, with no name indicated, and before payment of local development (infrastructure and services) taxes. Precedes issuance of a CRUH (see below).
Lettre d'attribution (see definition in note b) *Lettre de notification* (issued by communes)[b]	Since 2002, the lettre de notification testifies that a plot has been allocated by a commune. Payment of local development (infrastructure and services) taxes and submission of many documents must be made before the issuance of a CUH (see below)
PRECARIOUS TITLES	**THESE TITLES GIVE USE RIGHTS**
Concession rurale (CR [rural concession]). Issued on farmland by DRDC or a representative of the state whose level depends on the size of the plot.	Farmland must be developed within five years or the land may be taken back. In principle, CRs should not be granted within Bamako District, but it happens that they are.
	Annual fee must be paid.
	Possible transformation into ownership title after *immatriculation* (registration of the land under the name of the state).
Concession rurale à usage d'habitation (CRUH). Issued by rural communes.	A CRUH is issued after payment of local development taxes (for infrastructure and services). Land must be developed within three years. If it is not, the land can be taken back.
Concession urbaine d'habitation (CUH). Issued by urban communes.	A CUH can be delivered after the issuance of a lettre de notification and the payment of local development taxes (for infrastructure and services) to the commune, which must transfer 10 percent of these taxes to the state budget.
	Land must be developed within three years. If it is not, the land can be taken back. This precarious title may be transformed into an ownership title if the commune has obtained an ownership title from the state.
TITLES ISSUED BEFORE 2002, NOW THEORETICALLY TREATED AS CUH OR CRUH BUT STILL IN CIRCULATION	
Lettre d'attribution[b] (LA). Allocation letter issued by the governor of Bamako District or by prefects before 2002. *Permis d'occuper* (PO). Occupancy permit, issued by prefects before 2002.	Precarious title conditional on development of the land. If it is not, the land can be taken back. The prefect of Kati cercle continued issuing occupancy permits until 2009 although he no longer had the right to do so.

Table 3.1 (continued)

Documents or titles involving representatives of the state or communes and DRDC[a]	Characteristics
OWNERSHIP TITLES	**THESE TITLES GIVE OWNERSHIP RIGHTS**
Ownership title (issued by DRDC, state representatives)	Granted after confirming that land covered by CR, CRUH, and CUH has been developed.
	Registration fees of 15 percent of plot price must be paid to the state.

Note: CRUH = concession rurale à usage d'habitation (rural concession for residential purposes); CUH = concession urbaine d'habitation (urban concession for residential purposes); DRDC = Direction régionale des domaines et du cadastre (Regional Directorate of State Domains and of the Land Register).
a. The Direction nationale des domaines et du cadastre (DNCD) has a representative office in each region (DRDC). DRDC branch offices in Koulikoro region have been established in the cercles of the region and communes of Bamako District. Within these branch offices, the *bureau spécialisé* [specialist section] deals with precarious titles. The *bureau ordinaire* [ordinary section] deals with ownership titles.
b. The document that provides evidence that a plot has been allocated to a household. It is difficult to place the lettre d'attribution with certainty in either the administrative document category or the precarious title category, because this term seems frequently to be used to designate a lettre de notification. The issuance of lettres d'attribution should have come to an end in 2002 because the law of February 12, 2002, amending the Land Code of 2000 specifies that "Land allocations in the form of lettres d'attribution or permis d'occuper [occupancy permit] prior to the entry into force of this Code shall be treated as concessions urbaines or rurales à usage d'habitation." According to this text, lettres d'attribution should be considered as precarious titles. However, informants for this study often speak of them whereas they never mention the lettre de notification, an essential document for obtaining a CUH and concerning which the decree of March 6, 2002, specifies, "In no case may a lettre de notification stand in the stead of a use right title." If the mention of a lettre d'attribution actually refers to a lettre de notification, then the lettre d'attribution is an administrative document.

Only holders of ownership titles, known in Mali as titres fonciers, enjoy full, absolute ownership. Security of tenure should logically increase with moves toward obtaining ownership title and greater compliance with the rules relating to transactions; in reality, security also depends on other factors such as (1) social recognition: a household whose plot is in a village or neighborhood where everyone knows them can expect some solidarity from the neighbors if their occupation is called into question; (2) registration of transfers, particularly in cases of inheritance; (3) mobilization, often organized by associations, of communities threatened with eviction; (4) relations with the administration and political authorities, particularly political parties; and (5) land prices because the high monetary value of certain land can induce attempts at land grabbing. In addition, the validity of documents and titles, including ownership titles, is often challenged, giving rise to many conflicts (see "The Conflicts in the Land Delivery System" section in chapter 4).

The total number of precarious titles issued in Mali cannot be quantified. Collecting such figures from administrative sources would be possible but extremely difficult in practice. Some indicative figures concerning the number of land-owning households with ownership titles or land with ownership titles are available for Bamako District and Kati *cercle* (an administrative jurisdiction that includes several communes). The number of households in Mali who are owners of a plot or land with an ownership title is available from the 2009 census: 117,897, or 8.5 percent of all "owners." This percentage is higher in urban areas (27.7 percent). Data are available by region and for Bamako District where 36,896 households have an ownership title (30.6 percent of "owner households") but data are not available for Kati cercle. In that cercle, according to Djiré (2013), the number of plots with an ownership title has increased almost fivefold between the beginning of 2005 (14,314) and the end of 2012 (66,988). The author notes a sharp acceleration in 2011 and 2012. The trend stepped up even more during 2013 and the first quarter of 2014, as the number of plots with ownership titles rose to 87,945 as of April 15, 2014.[1]

Table 3.1 shows that there is a gap between lawful and actual practices. In this context, official documents alone (see annex 3A for laws, decrees, and other texts on land and tenure) cannot provide a sufficient understanding of the land tenure situation of a specific plot. Therefore, particular attention has been given to actual practices. Interviews with informants, including with agents in charge of land administration, reveal that they did not always agree on the meaning of terms used to describe land tenure situations.

The channels are represented in figures 3.1, 3.2, and 3.3, which highlight the different stages in the process to be followed to obtain an ownership title. This process does not generally involve the first buyer of the land and does not depend only on what individuals do, because public authorities may carry out tenure regularization operations. Generally, the process is interrupted by a sale: the new buyer can move forward with improvement and sell the land before obtaining a precarious title or ownership title, and the same can happen when further sales are made. Moreover, setbacks in the process can occur: for example, when the holder of an administrative document dies and the transfer of the plot is not registered, the heirs may well possess the land but have no documents in their names.

The Customary Land Delivery Channel

Customary Tenure in Mali

Customary land "ownership" refers to the communal possession of rights to use and allocate cropping and grazing land by a group sharing the same cultural identity. Land is passed on from generation to generation and considered sacred. The land chief[2] is responsible for the allocation, in the name of the group, of use rights to which members of the clan or lineage have a priority claim but which can be granted to people from outside the village, without any monetary transaction, in exchange for allegiance or verbal recognition of the debt. Outsiders have gradually succeeded in obtaining land in exchange for gifts or a sum of money. During the past two decades, customary land management practices have undergone various adjustments (Toulmin and Quan 2000). In most countries, customary practices have proved to have a surprising capacity to adapt to the new economic and social context introduced by the globalization of national economies and to the rapid spatial expansion of urban areas.

In Mali today, customary land is relatively scarce within Bamako District, where most of it has already been sold, but it is still abundant in peri-urban rural communes and in the rural hinterland of the city. In Bamako District, the outlying neighborhoods have extended into land that had been granted in the past by rural village chiefs to newcomers. The neighborhood chief, who is appointed by newcomers, plays the role of mediator between newcomers and the village land chief. Bourdarias (1999) describes this process in Dianguinabougou neighborhood in the north of Bamako commune I, observing that in the 1990s the rights of the land chiefs, by now extinguished in densely populated areas, were being maintained on land located beyond that built-up area, particularly in the territory of rural villages where some land had been sold. In Kati cercle, in the territory of Baguineda commune studied by Bouju and others (2009), families belonging to the community manage to sell the land they hold. The land chief, who is also the village chief, no longer has any other role than checking the validity of sales. In Soro village in the same commune, Becker (2013) observes that the right of families belonging to the lineages that first occupied the land to sell it seems to be implicitly recognized.

Customary tenure is recognized in Article 43 of the 2000 Land Code (*Code Domanial et Foncier*), which states that individual or collective customary rights holders cannot be deprived of these rights, except in the public interest and with fair compensation (Djiré and Traoré 2008). However, the implementing provisions of the Land Code have not yet been adopted. This issue was addressed at the National Land Convention (*États généraux du foncier* [République du Mali 2010]), but no decision has been made with regard to the formal recognition of customary tenure and transferability of customary rights. The state may register customary land under its own name (*immatriculation*); in practice, it will "purge" customary rights, meaning that it offers no compensation for the loss of the land but only for the loss of standing crops and other improvements made to the land. Upon registration under the name of the state, people occupying land with authorization from customary landholders but who have no written documents are not entitled to compensation. They may, however, be allowed to regularize their occupancy and then fall into the category of people using the public land delivery channel to access land (see "The Public and Parapublic Land Delivery Channel" later in this chapter).

Although customary ownership is legally recognized in rural areas in Mali, most customary landholders have no documents to guarantee their rights. Customary legitimacy is based on length of occupancy and the collective memory that places much value on oral agreements.

Sales of Customary Land

Explicit threats of expropriation or confiscation of customary land in peri-urban areas by state representatives, along with pressures from local authorities (who propose resettlement of households evicted following settlement upgrading and tenure regularization within Bamako District) and the hope of obtaining a good price, encourage customary landholders to subdivide their land, to sell it to developers and *coxers*,[3] or to accept land subdivisions made by prefects (see below). This very common practice has been observed in all the villages visited in the peri-urban area of Bamako. It contributes to land speculation and is a factor of corruption in land administration. Farther away from Bamako, villagers are reluctant to talk about these sales that compromise the sacred character of land. Speaking of his fieldwork, Becker (2013, p. 120) observes: "No one seemed comfortable with land sales, even those making sales spoke of it with unease or defensiveness. Land sales were contested, even within the founding lineage."

Today, there are four main ways customary land is transferred to buyers in the peri-urban areas and the rural hinterland of Bamako:[4]

1. The sale of customary land to individuals who will use it for agricultural purposes. They may subdivide it at a later stage to sell plots (see the third point).

2. The subdivision of the land and sale of individual land plots by customary landholders themselves. Although illegal, this practice, which is sometimes called customary *lotissement*,[5] enables the buyer to pay much less for the plot[6] than by approaching the commune or state authorities (see 3.2.1) and may lead to the issuance of a precarious title after a complex, time-consuming, and costly administrative procedure. Customary landholders often go through an intermediary, who may be a young person from a village family and who will pay himself handsomely for his participation in the plot subdivision. Customary landholders may ask the DRDC for a *concession rurale* (CR; rural concession) (see annex 3B) and then subdivide the land into plots and sell them on. However, in view of the lack of proper land information systems, the unavailability of subdivision layout plans, poor land management capacity at the commune level, and widespread clientelism, and given the poor quality of land transaction records kept at the local level (villages and communes), a series of illicit practices and disputes between sellers and

buyers can arise, especially when the same plot is the subject of multiple allocations to several different buyers at once.

3. The sale of large tracts of customary land (as opposed to individualized plots) to investors, cooperatives,[7] potential developers, and speculators for further subdivision, which occurs in the rural hinterland up to about 50–70 kilometers from Bamako city center. The buyer of the land may then apply for a CR by presenting an agricultural project and, in a later stage, subdivide it into plots and sell them on. This subdivision is not authorized; it creates a private, informal lotissement. The buyer may also go further in the tenure formalization process and obtain, after a CR, an ownership title. Then, after getting the approval of the regional director of urban planning and housing and the authorization of the governor of the region, the buyer will subdivide the land and sell the plots with an individual ownership title. It creates an authorized private *lotissement* (see "The Formal Private Land Delivery Channel" later in this chapter). Sales of large tracts of customary land in peri-urban rural communes can be easily formalized because of the financial means and social connections of powerful investors in land administration institutions.

4. Prefectoral lotissements, which are, in fact, a kind of land-sharing and subdivision scheme found in all rural communes in the peri-urban areas of Bamako in Kati cercle with the support of prefects and subprefects. In a prefectoral lotissement, customary land is surveyed and subdivided into three categories with, generally, the following breakdown:
   - Original customary holders who receive *bulletins* (a form of administrative recognition of the subdivision and proof of the allocation of land validated by the prefect or subprefect) retain 40 percent of the land. In some cases the customary holder may be allocated a *concession rurale à usage d'habitation* (CRUH; rural concession for residential purposes; see annex 3B) for the land he gets. If he applies for an ownership title, it may cost him the equivalent of 75 percent of the value of the land that has been returned to him following the subdivision. At the end of the process, if selling part of the land to pay for the ownership title, customary landholders will find themselves with an ownership title covering only 10 percent of the land they owned originally under the customary regime (Sanankoroba village, Sanankoroba commune, interview on June 4, 2011).
   - Another 40 percent is usually shifted to the prefect or subprefect, who will subdivide it into building plots that are, in principle, allocated mainly to households displaced following urban settlement upgrading (see "The Public and Para-Public Land Delivery Channel" later in this chapter). In principle, those to whom allotments are made receive a bulletin. The name of the holder is left blank.[8] The allottees may subsequently get their

name on the bulletin by paying the charges to have the land administration process their application and deliver them a precarious title (CRUH). They may also keep the bulletin, still with no name, and, without paying local taxes, sell the plot to someone who may not register it in his own name. In some cases, customary landholders receiving compensation in the form of plots may obtain a CRUH on those plots instead of a bulletin. A prefectoral *lotissement* is not legal but is very common. Remaining plots are sold at market price. The difference between market price and administration-set price[9] is frequently diverted by the prefect or subprefect. This is one of the reasons the state is so reluctant to transfer land management and land allocation responsibilities to commune authorities. The land that is shifted to the prefects enters the public land delivery channel after lotissement and follows a path relatively similar to what happens with plots allocated by communes (see "Administrative Allocation of Residential Plots in Authorized Lotissements and Lotissements with Regularization" later in this chapter).

- The land surveyor, who is paid in kind, is allocated 20 percent of the land, and will generally sell the plots.

Shifting from Customary Rights to Precarious and Ownership Titles

Depending on buyers' strategies, and on their investment capacity and on location, the customary land they buy can remain as is (that is, undeveloped or used for agricultural purposes), can be developed without subdivision (for an investment made by the buyer in an agricultural project), or can be subdivided into smaller plots (for agricultural or housing purposes). These plots may subsequently be the subject of a regularization operation.

In all cases, to improve tenure security—and under certain conditions, to improve the transferability of the land—the buyer can, as a first step, apply for a precarious title (CR).[10] The issuance of a CR is a complicated procedure involving a large number of administrations at local and central government levels (details about the procedure are given in annex 3B). Having a CR makes it possible to obtain, at a later stage, an ownership title. However, this is a time-consuming and costly process, which requires that CR holders develop their land within five years and pay very high fees. Corruption also makes the process troublesome and costly: some people who own a CR and have not made any investment manage to achieve regularization and obtain an ownership title within three months, while others who have a CR and have developed the land as required by the law cannot obtain an ownership title even after 10 years. In practice, most customary landholders have limited scope to transform a CR into an ownership title because they have neither the required financial resources nor sufficient connections within the land administration.[11] It can happen that a customary landholder will barter the land to a buyer for a piece of land with an ownership title. In that case, the buyer will deal with the formalities and costs of obtaining a master ownership title covering all the land and have an individual ownership title issued for the portion due to the customary holder. At the end of the process, the customary holder finds himself with an ownership title in respect of land representing no more than 10 percent of the area of customary land sold, similar to the practice described above in prefectoral lotissements.

Obtaining an ownership title is very profitable. With it, land can be sold at a much higher price, commonly up to three or four times that of land bought with a mere authenticated certificate of sale (for a definition, see annex 4A). According to informants, in the Dialakorodji commune, the price is multiplied by three; in Kanadjiguila village, in the Mandé commune, by four; and in Kalabancoro commune by five,[12] which makes rent capture possible for agents of the administration and beneficiaries of an ownership title.

The issuance of a CR on farmland encourages privatization of customary land. A study conducted in the rural municipality of Sanankoroba, 30 kilometers from Bamako, shows that Malian farmers are being excluded from official land ownership. Ownership of valuable lands is increasingly concentrated in the hands of public servants and entrepreneurs living in town (Djiré 2004). Authorities also increasingly see the issuance of CRs as one of the causes of urban sprawl,[13] which is one of the reasons the Council of Ministers decided to suspend the issuance of CRs in 2011. Since then, in April 2013, a decree has reauthorized the issue of CRs but under new conditions that strengthen the powers of the central government.

Figure 3.1 and annex 3.2 illustrate the different operations that can be undertaken to obtain an ownership title for land initially purchased from a customary landholder. In most cases, buyers may not complete the whole formalization process and may keep the plot as it is, possibly improve its tenure, and sell it on the informal market. People who hold a plot for residential use may be able to benefit from a rehabilitation and regularization operation. Figure 3.1 also shows the possibility of registration of customary land under the name of the state after the "purge" of customary rights.

The Public and Parapublic Land Delivery Channel

Public land can be transferred in several ways: (1) the allocation of residential plots in lotissements initiated by the state or by communes on their land; (2) the recognition of an existing occupation of the land by public authorities through the regularization processes of communes' lotissements; (3) the allocation of

Figure 3.1 The Customary Land Delivery Channel

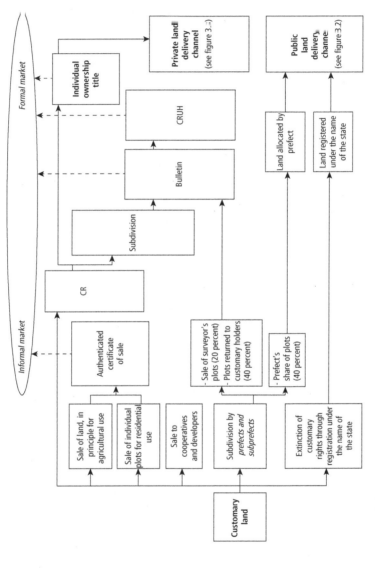

Note: CR = concession rurale (rural concession); CRUH = concession rurale à usage d'habitation (rural concession for residential purposes).

land through auction sale possibly after subdivision and provision of services; (4) the transfer or sale of land by the state to property development companies and cooperatives; and (5) the provision of land for social housing (see "Provision of Social Housing" later in this chapter).

Administrative Allocation of Residential Plots in Authorized Lotissements and Lotissements with Regularization

Before 1992, authorization for households to occupy plots on the private domain of the state was given by the governor of Bamako (the supervisory authority for the communes of Bamako). Beneficiary households would obtain a lettre d'attribution and had to build a house and pay local development taxes. Because demand for plots in Bamako was much greater than supply, people who were unable to find a place began to engage in "spontaneous settlements," which involved more than 45 percent of households by the early 1990s (Bertrand 2002). The question of regularization could no longer be ignored. At that time, the democratic transition with the drive toward decentralization of power led to changes in the way commune officials were chosen—with election replacing appointment by the central authorities—and in the procedure for regularizing occupation in Bamako District. Shortly afterward, with support from the World Bank, the land development agency (Agence de cession immobilière, or ACI) was set up and received very substantial allocations of land from the state in Bamako District, while a program to upgrade 24 informal settlements, known as Save our Neighborhood, was launched. The state retained ownership of the land in these 24 neighborhoods, but upgrading schemes were organized by the mayors of the communes. As part of a project to develop and service the neighborhood, municipal committees were to examine the situation of occupants of plots, and the communes would then either arrange regularization in place with a lettre d'attribution following payment of service and infrastructure charges or resettlement elsewhere in the commune on land set aside for that purpose; those resettled were often described as "evicted" (déguerpis). People who could not afford the service and infrastructure charges, which were very high in relation to the average income of Bamako residents, sold their plots (which was not allowed in principle) to others prepared to pay the charges in their stead (Bertrand 1998). Some communes took advantage of these operations to sell plots, against the rules, to well-placed individuals who, because they did not live in the neighborhood, could not claim regularization. Resettlement proved to be very difficult to implement because the designated areas were already occupied or had been allocated to ACI. Fearing further reductions in the areas under their control, some elected officials then stepped up the process of subdividing land they did not own (it belonged to the state) and sold plots despite not being entitled to do so.

The evaluation of the Save our Neighborhood program deemed the servicing of the neighborhoods to be completely inadequate. According to Mairie du District de Bamako (2010, p. 29), "the speculation that characterized the operation prevented the people who had been evicted from taking full advantage of the resettlement areas. Excluded from the resettlement process, these people simply reestablished their precarious lifestyle elsewhere" (translation from the original by the authors).

Since 2002, communes can carry out rehabilitation and tenure regularization operations, develop lotissements themselves, and allocate plots of land with precarious titles (CRUH and CUH) that can be transformed into ownership title (see annex 3C), provided that they have received an allocation of land from the state's private domain, which is only possible if the commune has a planning scheme approved by the Council of Ministers.[14] In practice, many communes do, without having ownership title, engage in rehabilitation and regularization operations in neighborhoods or villages in connection with lotissements, often at the request of residents on the land in question, and then come up against the state's land-ownership prerogatives or claims from holders of customary rights.[15] One example relating to the Samé neighborhood in Bamako commune III is reported in great detail by Leclerc-Olive and Keita (2004). Djiré (2004) describes the difficulties encountered by inhabitants of Sanankoroba commune in setting up a lotissement; Bakayoko (2005) presents the lotissement operations in three villages of Mandé commune and the conflicts they give rise to between village chiefs, communes, and state representatives. In these different cases, occupants of the land to be subdivided had contributed toward funding preparatory work in the hope of being able to deduct their contributions from the local development taxes to be paid on their plots. Carrying out a lotissement is a costly operation that requires the assistance of surveyors and various enterprises whom communes are tempted to reward by giving them plots in advance. These operations often involve local nongovernmental organizations that have links with foreign nongovernmental organizations likely to fund the preparatory work for the lotissement.

Households entitled to tenure regularization *in situ* receive an administrative document and can be granted a precarious title provided they have been able to pay the local development taxes for infrastructure and services and have submitted many other documents. This title cannot be transformed into ownership title if the commune has not received an allocation of land from the state.[16] In principle, plots can be taken back if holders of precarious titles do not develop them. However, assessing the development of plots (the land must be developed within three years for CUHs and CRUHs) is a somewhat arbitrary process carried out by officials of the Direction régionale des domaines et du cadastre (Regional Directorate of State Domains and of the Land Register) without objective criteria on which to base their assessment.[17] During the surveys conducted for this report, several holders of precarious titles in a commune in Kati cercle spoke of their fears of having their land taken back.

In practice, as in the 1990s, many beneficiary households do not obtain a precarious title because they cannot pay or because they sell the plot after receiving the lettre de notification. Households not entitled to regularization *in situ* must be resettled. Those who do not have any documents are at risk of not having access to any plot, either in place or in resettlement lotissements. Because land available for resettlement within Bamako District is scarce, households are being resettled in peri-urban rural communes.[18] It frequently happens that land allocation benefits households who are not entitled to it. It is a major source of revenue for mayors. An inspector of state property indicated that many people were in resettlement areas although they were not authorized to be resettled. A former senior official responsible for housing policy at the national level also stated that the allocation of resettlement plots, now a matter for mayors, was often undertaken to the benefit of people chosen by those mayors. He reckoned that about 60 percent of so-called resettlement plots were misappropriated for the benefit of people likely to vote for the mayor (see also box 4.2).

A widespread practice in any resettlement scheme in the urban or peri-urban areas of Bamako is to make more land plots available than are needed to resettle evicted households. The official reasons put forward by some involved mayors or prefects is that they must take the opportunity of resettlement projects to provide land to house the urban poor. However, some observers have said that the main purpose is to give them plots of land for housing that they can allocate to their clientele.

Land Allocation to the Parastatal Land Development Agency (ACI) for Auction Sale, Subdivision, and Development

The Agence de cession immobilière (ACI) was created in 1992 with the support of the World Bank. The objectives were and still are to put an end to the government monopoly on land by auctioning plots with an ownership title, to improve transparency in allocation procedures, and to develop a formal land market, which would supposedly improve access to land.

It sells plots by combining auctions and cross-subsidization to respond in principle to the demand from lower-middle to high-income groups, on a cost-recovery basis, so that land development projects can be replicated. In practice, however, ACI—to which large parts of the private domain of the state in Bamako (Bertrand 2002) had initially been allocated to the detriment of communes that were engaged, shortly afterward, in regularization operations—used the plots mainly to satisfy the demand from high-income groups[19] and did not provide enough land for the vast majority of the urban population, including emerging middle-income groups.

Bertrand (2002, p. 85) analyzes the failures of ACI as follows:

> ACI's sales management teams change regularly ... demonstrating [their] growing sensitivity ... to political patronage, just the kind of logic that donors had denounced in favor of the supposed purity of the market in the previous decade. The operation of auctions has been distorted due to sellers and buyers knowing each other and coming to various arrangements between themselves; public procurement processes for development have short-circuited competition to the benefit of over-the-counter agreements; accusations of misappropriation of funds are coming into sharp focus in 2000 to the extent that the agency is being challenged in court. The watchword of transparency is flagrantly flouted, after land-use management has been shown to result more than ever in social exclusion for the mass of impoverished citizens. (translation from the original by the authors)

Once sold by ACI, plots enter the private land delivery channel.

Many plots sold by ACI are not built on but held by speculators:

> Land bought at auction for one or two million CFA francs in 2000 can nowadays be sold on for several hundred millions. (Ville de Bamako 2012, p. 44; translation from the original by the authors)

Public Land Sold or Allocated to Private Property Development Companies and Cooperatives

The state may sell land with ownership title to approved property development companies. The companies then subdivide it, thus creating private formal lotissements, after obtaining administrative approvals. Similarly, the state may allocate land from its private domain to cooperatives. For an explanation of how these companies and cooperatives then operate downstream in the formal private land delivery channel, see the relevant subsections of "The Formal Private Land Delivery Channel" section.

Provision of Social Housing

The social housing program is aimed, in principle, at helping households access property ownership. It was initiated in 2003 by the government of Mali to respond to the needs of the middle-income groups that could afford neither land in ACI development schemes nor serviced land or housing put onto the market by formal private property developers.[20] So far, it has provided a relatively small number of dwelling units[21] at a subsidized price on lease-to-purchase arrangements or bank loans. Implementation of these housing programs has been rushed.[22] The social housing program is usually carried out in connection with a public-private partnership, with the state providing a property development company with land. The report *Bamako 2030* (Ville de Bamako 2012) stresses the absence of collective facilities in these housing projects:

> All the new social housing developments are located on the edges of the city's built area. Because the new neighborhood frequently lacks collective facilities, residents must travel long distances to go to school or to the market or fetch water from the nearest water point (Ville de Bamako 2012, p. 46; translation from the original by the authors)

Finally, it must be noted that, under cover of providing social housing, allocations are routinely the result of political patronage.

Figure 3.2 represents the public and parapublic land delivery channel. It shows in particular the different processes whereby the holder of a plot in a lotissement, which was originally allocated by public authorities, may obtain an ownership title. As in the customary land delivery channel, this is not a linear, irreversible process. Moreover, account must be taken here of the fact that it is not possible, at least while complying with legal procedures, to transform a precarious title into ownership title when the plot is in an unauthorized lotissement. Figure 3.2 also shows allocations and sales of land by the state to private property development companies, cooperatives, and ACI with an ownership title and highlights links between public delivery channels and customary and private delivery channels.

The Formal Private Land Delivery Channel

The bulk of the plots in the formal private land delivery channel directly derive from public and customary land delivery channels, as described above. The rest derive from sales made by individuals who may receive land for free from the state or who have been able to obtain it through the customary or public channels before getting an ownership title. Plots are sold on the formal land market.

Approved Private Property Development Companies

Private property development companies can obtain land from the state with an ownership title (see figure 3.2) or buy it either with an ownership title on the formal market or, without title, in the customary land delivery channel.

Figure 3.2 The Public and Parapublic Land Delivery Channel

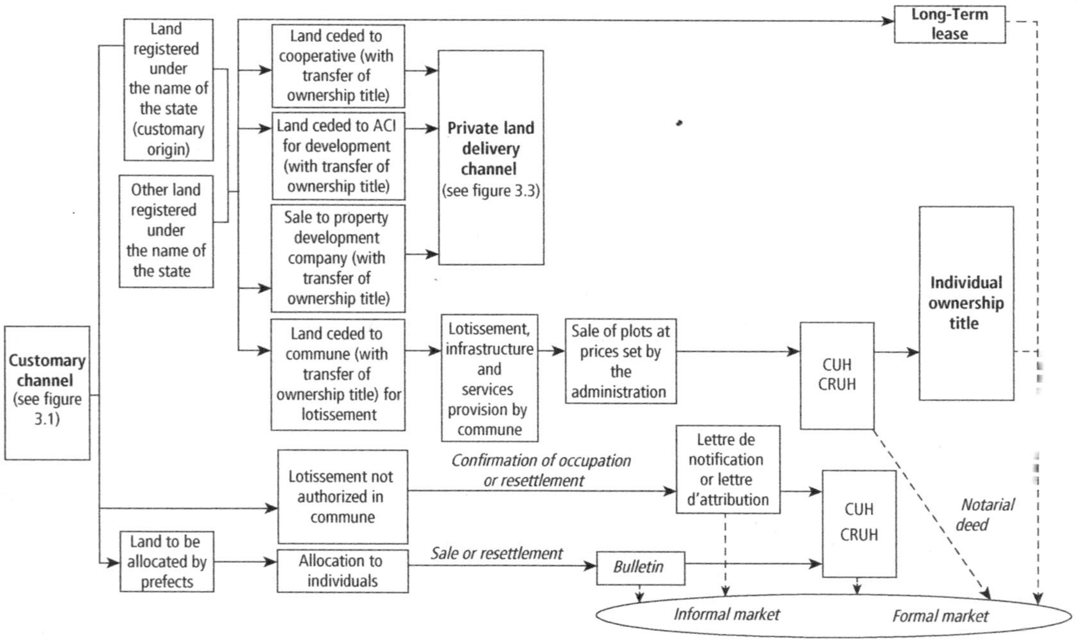

Note: CR = concession rurale (rural concession); CRUH = concession rurale à usage d'habitation (rural concession for residential purposes).

In the latter case, these companies undertake the necessary formalities to obtain an ownership title. They then service and develop the land and sell the plots, and sometimes build houses. They may also purchase already-developed land from ACI.[23] Either the plots are sold with individual ownership titles or the ownership title must be extracted from the "master" title; the price being higher in the first case in comparison with the second, all else equal.

About 200 approved property developers operate in Mali, usually on a small scale, depending on business opportunities. A few large companies that are members of the Association of Real Estate Developers of Mali (*Association des promoteurs immobiliers du Mali*) have been set up and take part in operations in public-private partnerships for social housing. For decades, the land management and administration framework was not conducive to the development of a formal private land and housing development sector, but since 2002, property developers have been granted advantages.[24] Nevertheless, the activities of private developers remain limited by urban households' low and irregular income; complex procedures and restrictive standards constraining norms for planning, construction, and development; the weakness of the housing finance system (see box 3.1);

BOX 3.1

Weakness of the Housing Finance System

According to banking regulations, only ownership titles can be accepted as security for loans, but according to Law 02-008 of February 12, 2002, a precarious title transferred by a notarial deed can also be accepted as collateral provided that the notary commits to transform it into an ownership title. In practice, obtaining the ownership title may prove impossible and the bank will lose out in the event of a default.

There are many cases of fraud concerning titles pledged to obtain a loan. Borrowers may obtain overvalued fictitious certificates from so-called expert assessors; in this case the bank is at risk of never recouping the amount of the loan in case of default. In addition, it is difficult to correctly establish the value of mortgaged land. Assessments made by state-approved property experts may not be reliable.

It is also difficult for a bank to verify that those who request loans truly own the land in the absence of a land information system and given the unreliability of the land registry. Loans may also be requested for properties that will never be built.

In addition, banks lend at a high interest rate (between 10 percent and 12 percent), for an average term for a mortgage loan of 12–15 years, which further impedes the development of the formal market.

Source: Interview with managers of the Malian mortgage guarantee fund (September 2011).

uncertainties surrounding security of tenure even with an ownership title; the competition from ACI for the provision of serviced land for housing for the high-income group; the competition from the public land delivery channel; and competition from the informal sector. Property development companies also complain about their own difficulties in accessing land, particularly in the center of Bamako.

Land and property development companies that have bought customary land without title and for which they have subsequently obtained ownership title may come into conflict with the occupants of that land (see chapter 4).

Cooperative Housing

A cooperative can obtain land from the state (see figure 3.2) and then subdivide for its members;[25] it may also purchase customary land without title and then obtain an ownership title. Cooperatives were originally set up by trade unions (for example, Union des travailleurs du Mali) and by professional associations. Employees of public organizations may gain access to land through membership in cooperatives.[26] Cooperatives are also popular with Malians abroad, who may join together to buy land (for instance, Malians from the suburbs of Paris; see Keita 2012).

The distinction between private developers and cooperatives is not always clear; private developers sometimes operate under the name of "housing cooperatives."

In a similar formula, cooperative operations may also be launched by companies to house their employees. Some companies have obtained land subdivided by ACI (Bertrand 1995); others buy from individuals and complain about the costs they have to bear.

Gifts of Land with Ownership Title by the State

Some people may sell land or plots with ownership titles that they have obtained as a gift from the state (this applies particularly to military personnel before 1991). Some may arrange a *division parcellaire* and then sell the plots.[27]

The Secondary Formal Market

Some owners who have purchased land without title or with a precarious title that they have then transformed into an ownership title or who have purchased land directly with an ownership title can sell it on the formal market. Selling land with an ownership title is perfectly legal but expensive because the operation is subject to conditions: a notarial deed must be drawn up and registration fees must be paid, together with transfer charges.

These processes are represented in figure 3.3.

Figure 3.3 The Formal Private Land Delivery Channel

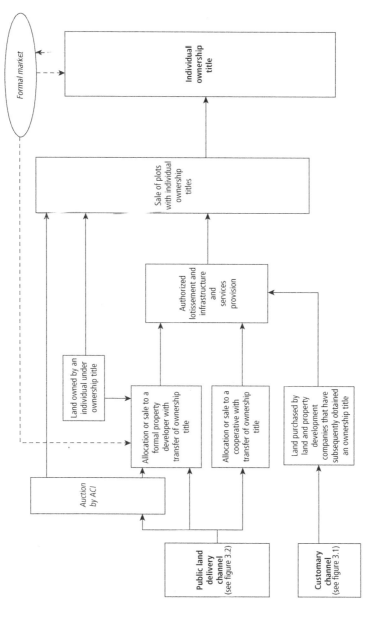

Note: ACI = Agence de cession immobilière (Land Development Agency).

Annex 3A Laws, Decrees, and Other Texts on Land and Tenure

- Décret n° 91-321/PM-RM du 3 octobre 1991, portant modalités d'application des dispositions du Code domanial et foncier relatives aux concessions rurales.

- Décret n° 91-322/PM-RM du 3 octobre 1991, portant réglementation des modalités et conditions des cessions des terrains domaniaux par adjudication publique.

- Décret n° 91-323/PM-RM du 3 octobre 1991, portant réglementation de la cession amiable des terrains domaniaux.

- Décret n° 91-324/PM-RM du 3 octobre 1991, portant organisation et modalités de fonctionnement de la commission chargée des évaluations foncières.

- Décret n° 92-113/PM-RM du 9 avril 1992, portant fixation des prix de cession et des redevances des terrains urbains et ruraux du domaine privé de l'État, à usage commercial, industriel et d'habitation.

- Décret n° 92-114/PM-RM du 9 avril 1992, portant fixation des barèmes généraux de base des prix de cession et des redevances des terrains ruraux appartenant à l'État et détermination des procédures d'estimation des barèmes spécifiques.

- Loi n° 95-034, du 12 avril 1995, portant Code des collectivités territoriales en République du Mali.

- Loi N° 96-025 du 21/02/1996, portant statut particulier du District de Bamako.

- Loi N° 96-050 du 16 octobre 1996, portant principes de constitution et gestion du domaine des Collectivités Territoriales.

- Loi N° 99-026 du 07 juillet 1999, portant ratification de l'ordonnance n° 99-003/P-RM du 31 mars 1999, portant création de la Direction Nationale des Collectivités Territoriales.

- Ordonnance n° 00-27 du 22 mars 2000, portant Code domanial et foncier.

- Décret n° 01-040/P-RM du 21 février 2001 déterminant les formes et conditions d'attribution des terrains du domaine privé immobilier de l'Etat.

- Décret n° 01-041/P-RM du 21 février 2001, fixant les modalités d'attribution du permis d'occuper.

- Loi n° 02-008 du 12 février 2002, portant modification et ratification de l'ordonnance n° 00-027/P-RM du 22 mars 2000, portant code domanial et foncier.

- Décret n° 02-113/P-RM du 6 mars 2002, fixant les modalités d'organisation et de confection du Cadastre.

- Loi n° 01-077 du 18 juillet 2001, fixant les règles générales de la construction.

- Décret n° 02-114 P-RM du 06 mars 2002, portant fixation des prix de cession et des redevances des terrains urbains et ruraux du domaine privé de l'État, à l'usage commercial, industriel, artisanal, de bureau, d'habitation ou autres.

- Décret n° 02-115 P-RM du 06 mars 2002, portant fixation des barèmes généraux de base des prix de cession, des redevances des terrains ruraux appartenant à l'État et détermination de la procédure d'estimation des barèmes spécifiques.

- Décret n° 02-111 et 112/P-RM du 22 mars 2002, déterminant les formes et les conditions de gestion des terrains des domaines publics immobiliers de l'Etat et des collectivités territoriales.

- Loi n° 02-016 du 3 juillet 2002, fixant les règles générales d'urbanisme.

- Décret n° 05-113/P-RM du 9 mars 2005, fixant les règles spécifiques applicables aux différentes catégories de servitudes en matière d'urbanisme.

- Décret n° 05-114/P-RM du 9 mars 2005, déterminant les modalités de réalisation, de gestion et de normalisation des infrastructures urbaines.

- Décret n° 05-115/P-RM du 9 mars 2005, fixant les modalités de réalisation des différents types d'opérations d'urbanisme.

- Décret n° 10-176/PM-RM du 25 mars 2010, fixant le cadre institutionnel de pilotage du quatrième Projet urbain du Mali.

- Lettre circulaire interministérielle n° 2011-001/MATCI-MLAFU-SG du 31 octobre 2011, relative à la suspension des attributions du domaine privé immobilier de l'Etat (suite au Conseil des ministres du 15 juin 2011).

- Loi du 15 Décembre 2011 (dite Loi Hamidou Diabaté), portant modification de l'ordonnance n° 00-027 du 22 mars 2000, portant code domanial et foncier modifiée et ratifiée par la loi n° 02-008 du 12 Février 2002.

- Décret N° 2013-341/PRM du 18 avril 2013, portant modification du Décret N° 01-040/P-RM du 02 février 2001, déterminant les formes et conditions d'attribution des terrains du domaine privé immobilier de l'Etat.

Annex 3B Details of Required Procedures and Costs of Formalization from Customary Land to Ownership Title

Type of operation	Procedures[a]	Participants[a]	Costs of the operation (excluding undeclared payments)
Sale of customary land to a private individual who keeps the land and may obtain precarious title (CR) and then ownership title	Stage 1. Authentication of the sale: Issuance of an authenticated certificate of sale by mayor's office	– Buyer and seller – Coxer (informal broker), surveyor, and village's authorities – Mayor's office	– Purchase price of land – Payments to coxer and surveyor – Fee due to mayor's office

	Stage 2. Application for CR:
	– Plotting by authorized surveyor[b]
	– Confirmation by DRDC[c] that no ownership title exists
	– Application to state representatives according to surface area of land
	– Public inquiry announced in newspaper then record of discussion and administrative certificate signed by state representative
	– Allocation of CR with specifications on development requirements.
		– Surveyors
		– DRDC
		– Various levels of central government:
		  – Subprefect if <2.5 ha[c]
		  – Prefect if 2.5–5 ha,
		  – Governor if 5–10 ha,
		  – Minister of State Domains if 10–100 ha,
		  – Council of Ministers if > 100 ha
		– Village communities
		– All interested parties in the vicinity
			– Payment to authorized surveyor (who may have the work done by an unauthorized surveyor)
			– Local development taxes and annual tax

	Stage 3. Application for ownership title: – Development within five years or land may be taken back – *Immatriculation* under the name of the state – Allocation by DRDC[c] with data recorded in the Livre foncier (Land book)	– DRDC	– Registration fees of 15 percent of the price of the land

(continued next page)

Type of operation	Procedures[a]	Participants[a]	Costs of the operation (excluding undeclared payments)
Sale of customary land to a private individual who will arrange subdivision and sell the resultant plots. The plot holders may obtain a precarious title (*concession rurale à usage d'habitation*, or CRUH) and apply for an ownership title provided that the plot is in an authorized *lotissement* (Ownership title has previously been awarded to the commune)	Stage 1. Same as stage 1 above	Same as stage 1 above	Same as stage 1 above
	Stage 2. Same as stage 2 above	Same as stage 2 above	Same as stage 2 above
	Stage 3. Application to prefect for authorization to subdivide as previously recommended by surveyor: − For each plot, the prefect's office prepares bulletin − Sale of plots with bulletin often with aid of *coxer*	− Surveyor − Prefect	− Cost of surveyor − Charges for bulletin: CFAF 80,000–300,000 − Cost of coxer
	Stage 4. Transformation of bulletin into CRUH: − Bulletin put in buyer's name and application for CRUH sent to the commune by the buyer − Conditions: Buyer must not possess another residential lot in the same commune and must have tax receipt − Decision subject to signature by the mayor, who will issue notification of allocation and seek payment of the fees − Registration of the title in the register of CRUHs	− Prefect or subprefect − Mayor's office after opinion from village council meeting for the purpose, endorsed by resolution from commune council	− Local development (infrastructure and services) taxes vary according to commune; 19 percent of these taxes are for the state budget.
	Stage 5. Transformation of CRUH into ownership title: − Certificate of development issued by branch office of the DRDC[c] − Deposit of copy of CRUH that will be cancelled − Copy of ownership title handed to interested party − Recording of ownership title in the *Livre foncier* [Land book]	− Mayor's office: Assessment of development − Ordinary section of the DRDC branch office in the commune	− Registration fees of 15 percent of plot price

Note: CR = concession rurale (rural concession); CRUH = concession rurale à usage d'habitation (rural concession for residential purposes); DRDC = Direction régionale des domaines et du cadastre (Regional Directorate of State Domains and of the Land Register); CFAF = CFA franc; ha = hectares.

a. Changes since 2011 and other changes after April 2013 (see annex 3.1).

b. Note that 90 percent of land demarcations are carried out without the consent of all parties involved according to reliable sources at the Department of Agricultural Engineering. This practice generates land disputes.

c. The Direction nationale des domaines et du cadastre (National Directorate of State Domains and of the Land Register) has representation in each region (DRDC); for this study, the Koulikoro regional office. Local branch offices have been set up in the cercles and communes. Within these branch offices, the specialized section deals with precarious title and the ordinary section with ownership title.

Annex 3C Details of Required Procedures and Costs of Formalization from Allocations by the State or Communes to Acquire Individual Ownership Title

Type of operation	Procedures	Participants	Costs incurred
Land of the state's private domain transferred to a commune, which allocates it to private individuals in connection with an authorized lotissement	Stage 1. Assignment from the state's private domain to the commune that has a planning document and wishes to carry out a lotissement: – Decision made by the Council of Ministers following application from the commune – The ownership title is transferred to the commune with prior verification that there is no ownership title other than that held by the state to the requested land.	– Council of Ministers on submission from the minister for state domains – The commune consults residents and often acts at their request	n.a.
	Stage 2. Application for precarious title (CUH or CRUH) sent to the commune by the occupant of the plot – Condition: nonpossession of another residential lot in the same commune and possession of tax receipt – Opinion from the village, fraction of neighborhood, or municipal council – In case of bare land >1,000 square meters, approval of state representatives required – Decision subject to signature by the mayor, who will issue notification of allocation and seek payment of the fees – Registration of the title in the register of CUHs or CRUHs. Specifications approved by municipal council, especially development.	– Village, fraction of neighborhood, or mayor – Various levels of central government: – Prefect if 1,000–5,000 square meters – Governor if 5,000 square meters to 1 ha – Minister for local authorities if 1–5 ha – Council of Ministers if >5 ha – Specialized section of the DRDC branch office in the commune	– Local development (infrastructure and services) taxes varying according to commune; 10 percent of the taxes are for the state budget
	Stage 3. Application for ownership title: – Condition: Development on terms imposed by each commune or threat to take back land – Striking out of development clause – Application for ownership title to land registry office in place where the building is located – Deposit of the copy of CUH or CRUH that will be cancelled – Recording of ownership title in the *Livre foncier* [Land book]	– Mayor's office: Assessment of development – Ordinary section of the DRDC branch office	– Registration fees (15 percent of the plot price)

Note: CRUH = concession rurale à usage d'habitation (rural concession for residential purposes); CUH = concession urbaine d'habitation (urban concession for residential purposes); DRDC = Direction régionale des domaines et du cadastre (Regional Directorate of State Domains and of the Land Register); ha = hectares; n.a. = not applicable.

Notes

1. The source of this information is the Kati cercle branch of the Direction des domaines et du cadastre.
2. The functions of village chief and land chief are not necessarily exercised by the same person.
3. "Coxers" are land brokers who operate on informal land markets throughout the Bamako area and to whom many buyers and sellers resort to transact land. They have informers in peri-urban villages to identify land that can be transacted and negotiate with village authorities; therefore, they are key players in the rural-to-urban conversion process. They are also aware of the "tricks" that can be used to circumvent regular procedures and deal with the administration to make sales effective. They are often found in publicly visible places, including on the side of roads not far from plots that are for sale.
4. Before 1991, according to informants for this study, the state allocated land of customary origin, which it had registered under its own name, to its clientele (army and police officers, senior government officials). Some of this land has since been sold on to individuals or investors.
5. The term *lotissement* is often misused. According to Decree No. 05-115 of March 9, 2005 (which establishes the procedures for carrying out the different types of urban development operations), a *lotissement* is "the subdivision of a single piece of bare land into plots with appropriate provision of infrastructure and collective facilities to host the buildings to be erected by the future occupants." According to the decree, the lotissement requires the prior issuance of an ownership title, the approval of the regional director of urban planning and housing, and the authorization of the governor of the region or of the district for Bamako. Infrastructure and collective facilities are specified as "roads, drains/sewers, water supply, electricity and telephone." Field work conducted for this study showed that both residents and the authorities use the same word *lotissement* as a catchall term that refers to a wide range of land subdivisions. Some are legal and authorized, others are not. The various categories of lotissement are presented in the text.
6. In Moribabougou commune, Kati cercle, in the 1980s, a sum 10 times higher had to be paid for a plot allocated by the prefect than for a plot allocated by the village chief, who might even issue a lettre d'attribution, quite illegally (Béridogo 2003).
7. We were told, for instance, that the cooperative of *gendarmes* (a police corps that is part of the national armed forces) in the village of Missalabougou, Kalabancoro commune, in Kati cercle, illustrates this kind of operation.
8. According to the rules, only communes can grant CRUHs. In practice, prefects grant them as well.
9. The administration-set price is the price set by an administrative decision. It refers to a price list established by government authorities in a given area. These prices are far below market prices and the lists are rarely updated.
10. A CR ensures a fair degree of security of tenure. Furthermore, land with a CR can be transferred under certain conditions.

11. There are, however, some special cases such as Soro village studied by Becker (2013): nonresidents from one of the village families can obtain land in exchange for gifts of money to the village and then obtain ownership title. One may wonder whether it is still possible to speak of customary rights holders in such cases.

12. Information from interviews with key informants in Bamako between June 2011 and January 2012 and Durand-Lasserve (2009).

13. The report *Bamako 2030* (Ville de Bamako 2012, p. 44) notes that farmland being sold with a concession rurale to "private individuals" who divide it up into residential plots is "a real threat because it encourages urban sprawl to the detriment of rural natural resources."

14. The first master plan and urban planning document (*Schéma Directeur d'Aménagement et d'Urbanisme*, or SDU) for Bamako was adopted in 1981. The third revised version dates from 2004 but has not yet been approved. Some peri-urban communes have also prepared planning documents, some of which have been approved by the Council of Ministers (joint SDU for Moribabougou and N'Gabakoro Droit in 2008; joint SDU for Dialakorodji, Safo, and Sangarabougou in 2010; SDU for Mountougoula and Sanankoroba in 2010).

15. According to the Direction régionale de l'urbanisme et de l'habitat of Bamako District, it is hard to know how many unauthorized lotissements there are. It estimates that, for example, between 70 percent and 80 percent of the lotissements in Bamako commune I are unauthorized.

16. In 2012, the DNDC asked all branch managers to cease issuing CUHs unless a planning document had been approved. This resulted in a sharp drop in numbers of CUHs granted, but the issuance of lettres de notification continued according to the Direction régionale de l'urbanisme et de l'habitat of Kati cercle.

17. Article 11 of Decree No. 02-114 P-RM of March 6, 2002 (see annex 3.1), sets out the conditions for allocating land from the territorial authorities' private domain: "Each authority shall set the conditions for, and development requirement of, the allocated plots according to specifications approved by the municipal council." According to an inspector of the state domains, this also depends on location. Where permanent structures are required, more than CFAF 1 million must be spent but, in some other areas, there is no requirement for permanent structures.

18. In this way, for example, resettlement areas for Bamako communes I and II were planned in N'Gabacoro and for commune V in Kalabancoro.

19. The purchase of several plots by the same person, although prohibited, was common (Bertrand 1998).

20. The origins of the policy lie in the provision of land to military personnel in 1992 by then-General Amadou Toumani Touré, hence the popular term "ATT-Bougou" (meaning "ATT neighborhood"). Private developers may also be involved and can obtain land from the state at attractive prices, or even for nothing, and build housing to be sold on credit.

21. According to the Ministry of Housing, Land Affairs and Urban Planning, 2,930 affordable housing units were put onto the market in Bamako between 2003 and 2007. During this period, registered demand at the national level was more than 30,000. The state provided 50 percent of the funding, with 35 percent coming from

the Malian Housing Agency and 15 percent from ACI. Some 10,000 additional housing units (including 5,400 financed by the state) were scheduled countrywide between 2008 and 2012. This objective was reassessed in 2010, with the announcement of the construction of an additional 20,000 units over the next four years.

22. The Focal Point for Urban Development, Ministry of Housing, Land Affairs and Urban Planning was requested in 2002 to urgently design a social and affordable housing program. After a week's work, its proposal (inspired by the experience of 300 housing units in Garantiebougou) was validated by the president and implemented with state funding. Subsequently, no other comprehensive study was done (ISTED 2009).

23. In March 2014, ACI and the Association des Promoteurs Immobiliers du Mali advertised the sale of 1,050 housing units in Dialakorobougou, Kati cercle, with the aim of establishing a new town ("Lancement commercial des 1050 logements de Dialakorobougou : l'ACI en partenariat avec APIM s'engage pour la création d'une nouvelle ville moderne," L'Indépendant, March 25, 2014).

24. By way of example, Decree No. 00-274/P-RM of June 23, 2000, permits the state to sell land from its private domain at preferential prices or allocate land free of charge, with a clause reserving ownership for the state, to developers planning to establish a number of "affordable social plots" or "very affordable" and "low-cost" housing units.

25. It may also buy land and, in that case, will often approach a customary holder directly before having the land subdivided. In this case, the transaction comes under the customary land delivery channel (see figure 3.1).

26. There were great expectations in the early 2000s that cooperative housing would improve affordability for middle-income groups.

27. A division parcellaire is the subdivision of a single piece of land into at most five plots, which in theory are not to be sold but are for donation or inheritance purposes (decree of March 9, 2005, Article 27). During the survey for this study, it was found that this rule had been ignored in some peri-urban communes of Bamako.

References

Bakayoko, I. 2005. "L'Afrique à l'épreuve de la décentralisation: Les enjeux de la transformation foncière, le cas du Mali." Presentation at the general assembly of CODESRIA (the Council for the Development of Social Science Research in Africa). Maputo, December 6–10.

Becker, L. 2013. "Land Sales and the Transformation of Social Relations and Landscape in Peri-Urban Mali." Geoforum 46: 113–23.

Béridogo, B. 2003. "Les interactions rurales et urbaines dans le site périurbain de Moribabugu (Mali)." Recherches Africaines, Annales de la Faculté des Lettres, Langues, Art et Sciences Humaines de Bamako, n° 2.

Bertrand, M. 1995. "Bamako, d'une République à l'autre." Annales de la Recherche Urbaine 66: 40–51.

———. 1998. "Marchés fonciers en transition: le cas de Bamako, Mali." Annales de Géographie 602: 381–409.

———. 2002. "Gestion foncière et logique de projet urbain: expériences comparées en Afrique occidentale, francophone et anglophone." *Historiens et Géographes* 379: 77–90.

Bouju, J., A. Ausseil, M. F. Ba, M. Ballo, H. Bocoum, and C. Touquent. 2009. "Dynamique des transactions foncières au Mali: Mountougoula, Baguinéda, centre ville de Bamako, Bandagiara et Niilgari." Report from IRAM (Institut de recherche et d' étude sur le monde arabe)/CEAMA (Centre d'étude et de recherche sur le monde arabe et méditerranéen), Paris/Aix en Provence.

Bourdarias, F. 1999. "La ville mange la terre: désordres fonciers aux confins de Bamako." *Journal des Anthropologues* 77–78: 141–60.

Djiré, M. 2004. "Mythes et réalités de la gouvernance locale: l' expérience de la commune rurale de Sanankoroba, Mali." Dossier 130, International Institute for Environment and Development, London.

———. 2013. "La ruée sur les terres péri-urbaines -un sujet supplémentaire d'inquiétude pour la gouvernance foncière au Mali." Paper prepared for the Annual World Bank Land and Poverty Conference, Washington, DC, April 8–11.

———, and K. Traoré. 2008. "Assurer la sécurisation légale des transactions foncières: quel rôle pour les intermédiaires et facilitateurs?" Études de cas en zones péri-urbaines et dans le Mali-Sud, Support to the Legal Empowerment of the Poor, Legal Empowerment in Practice – LEP Working Paper, Food and Agriculture Organization of the United Nations.

Durand-Lasserve, A. 2009. "Harmonisation des systèmes fonciers au Mali par une intégration du droit coutumier au droit formel." Programme d'appui aux collectivités territoriales (Division Gestion du foncier communal). GTZ Mali.

ISTED (Institut des sciences et des techniques de l' équipement et de l' environnement pour le développement). 2009. "Étude sur les pratiques de gouvernance urbaine." Étude de cas – Mali, technical report.

Keita, B. 2012. "Migrations internationales, investissements immobiliers et recomposition territoriale en Afrique de l'Ouest: le cas de Bamako." PhD dissertation, Université Paris VII Denis Diderot.

Leclerc-Olive, M., and A. Keita. 2004. "Les villes: laboratoires des démocraties?" Research report, PRUD (Programme de Recherche Urbaine pour le Développement)/ISTED (Institut des Sciences et des techniques de l' équipement et de l' environnement pour le Développement)/GEMDEV (Groupement d' intérêt scientifique pour l' étude de la Mondialisation et du Développement), Paris.

Mairie du District de Bamako. 2010. *Premier forum sur le développement urbain de Bamako*. Bamako, Mali.

République du Mali. 2010. "Rapport de Synthèse des Concertations des États Généraux du Foncier." Ministère du Logement, des Affaires Foncières et de l'Urbanisme, Commission Nationale d'Organisation des États Généraux du Foncier.

Toulmin, C., and J. Quan, eds. 2000. *Evolving Land Rights, Policy and Tenure in Africa*. London: International Institute for Environment and Development and Natural Resources Institute.

Ville de Bamako. 2012. *Bamako 2030: croissance et développement - Imaginer des stratégies urbaines pour un avenir maîtrisé et partagé*. Final report, Bamako.

Chapter 4

The Land Delivery System

Description of the Land Delivery System

It is clear from figures 3.1, 3.2, and 3.3 that the three land delivery channels form a system. Customary and public channels interact because the state can purge customary rights, register the land under its name, and may allocate it to the *communes* (administrative jurisdictions headed by a mayor) that engage in *lotissements*.[1] Communes may regularize occupation of customary land located in their territory, possibly following payment of compensation; and sell plots. The public and customary land delivery channels supply the land for the private formal land delivery channel. The three land delivery channels supply plots that may be sold on land markets. Figure 4.1 represents the entire land delivery system.

The three main characteristics of the land delivery system are the diversity of tenure situations and of land transfers (through allocations or sales), which may or may not be legal; the links between land delivery channels and the market; and the diversity of the stakeholders involved in the land delivery system.

Legality of Land Allocations, Titling, and Sales

Irregularities in Land Management

Land allocations in public land delivery are not always legal. It may happen that land administrations allocate *concessions rurales* (CRs; rural concessions) on land on which there is no agricultural activity. Furthermore, they also may illegally deliver *titres fonciers* [ownership titles].

According to the rules, state representatives should allocate CRs for agricultural land, whereas the allocation of precarious titles known as *concessions à usage d'habitation* (CUH; concessions for residential purposes, which may be urban or rural) is the responsibility of the communes. Actual practice is different. The Auditor General mentions in his 2011 Annual Report

Figure 4.1 The Land Delivery System

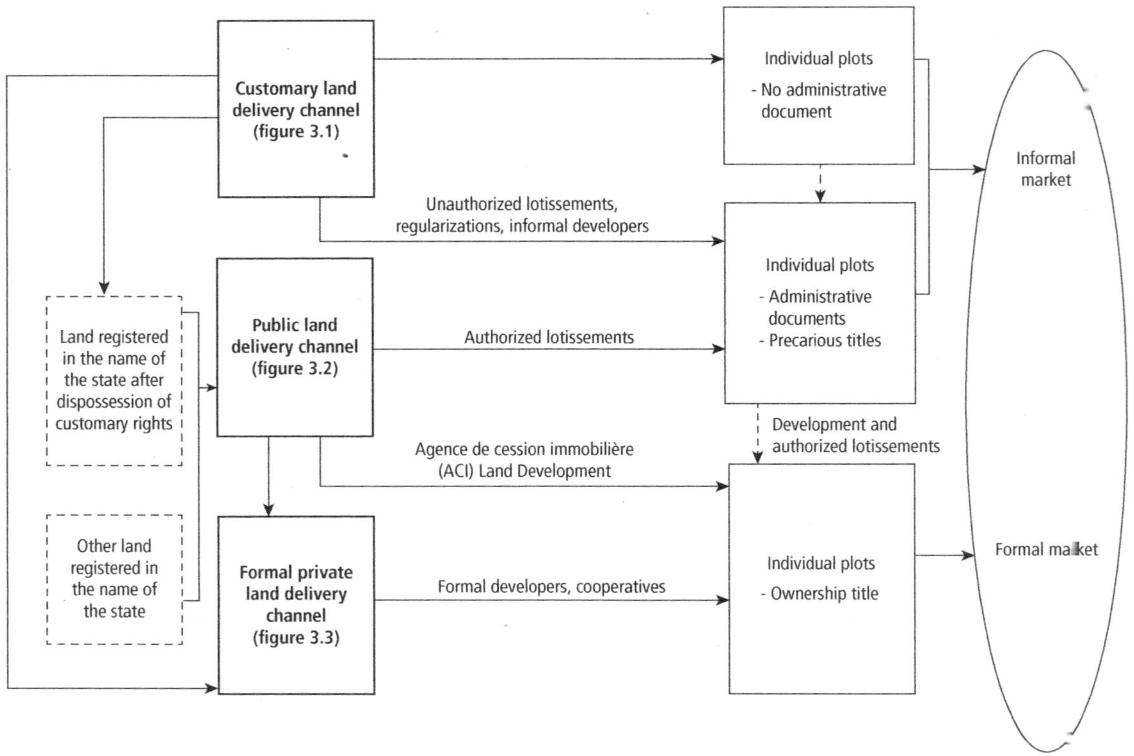

(République du Mali 2012, p. 61 that "Kati *cercle* (an administrative jurisdiction that includes several communes) is continuing, despite the absence of legal foundation, to allocate CUHs" (translation from the original by the authors).

Communes deliver *lettres d'attribution* (administrative documents that authorize the allottee to apply for a CUH on plots located in unauthorized lotissements).

It happens that some plots allocated by communes are located on public rights of way and spaces (green areas, public squares, and shopping facilities) in the "land pockets" of Bamako District, which results in a fair amount of conflicts, demolitions, and court proceedings (Bertrand 2012). An operation was announced in May 2014 to free the rights of way and other places in Bamako District.

Although communes and the local branch offices of the Direction régionale des domaines et du cadastre (Regional Directorate of State Domains and of the Land Register) should no longer allocate more than one plot for residential purposes to any one family (to encourage wider access to plots),[2] this is still common practice. The Auditor General's Annual Report for 2011 (République du Mali 2012, p. 54) notes, regarding Bamako District, that "The *Antenne* [branch office] of Commune IV, for example, registered multiple land allocations. During the period 2008–2010, several people were individually allocated between five and fourteen residential lots" (translation from the original by the authors). Certain state representatives grant CRs for land that is of a size more suited to housing. According to République du Mali (2012), the subprefect of the Kalabancoro region has granted CRs for very small plots (300 square meters) by subdividing customary land or land that had already been designated for a CR by the prefect. Moreover, the prefect of Kati cercle is said to have granted several CRs to the same person, which he is prohibited from doing.[3]

Forged Ownership Titles and Multiple Allocation of a Lettre d'Attribution for the Same Plot

In principle, an ownership title guarantees total security for its owner. In practice, forged ownership titles may be issued. Banks in particular report their reluctance to grant loans on the basis of these titles (see box 3.1). Doubts regarding the quality of ownership titles lead to conflicts. The situation can be complicated when the same piece of land is claimed both by housing cooperatives that say they obtained it from the state and by property companies, as has happened in Gouana, in Kati cercle.[4]

There are many inhabitants of Bamako and of Kati cercle who have lettres d'attribution (LA) for the same plot. Multiple LAs can happen in particular when beneficiaries of an LA do not know (or pretend not to know) the provision of the law that stipulates that the land must be developed within three years. Thus, someone who has held an LA for many years can transfer the plot without having developed it; meanwhile, a coxer (informal broker) may offer this same land to a buyer because it appears to be vacant. That buyer can then, with the complicity of the local authority, also obtain an LA. The identity of those taking up a precarious title is not always confirmed, as evidenced by the Auditor General in the 2011 report: "The *Antenne* [branch officer] of the *bureau specialisé* [specialist office] of commune IV also permitted the take-up of 811 CUHs by third parties without authority. By way of illustration, five of these people took up between 38 and 56 CUHs in 2009" (République du Mali 2012, p. 54; translation from the original by the authors).

The Hamidou Diabaté Law of December 2011 provides that litigation between the holder of a precarious title and the holder of an ownership title shall be subject exclusively to the jurisdiction of the courts of law. Previously, such litigation was heard by an administrative court, which had the power to investigate whether all the administrative procedures for the allocation of an ownership title had been followed. The dispute may now relate only to the terms of the contract between the buyer and the seller. There are many conflicts, however, between holders of precarious titles and ownership titles on the same piece of land, as illustrated by the example in box 4.1.

The Importance of Social Connections and Corruption

Allocation of plots by the communes is heavily dependent on social and political connections and clientelistic relations, which play an important part in Malian culture. Membership in the leading political party in the commune, or in an influential trade union or association, or links with a nongovernmental organization working on servicing land in the commune can be determining factors in obtaining a plot, regularizing tenure, and speeding up the process of

---

BOX 4.1

Ownership Title against Precarious Title to the Same Plot of Land

In the N'Tabacoro area in Mandé commune, the state granted an ownership title for the construction of social and affordable housing on land covered by precarious titles previously granted by prefects but refused to compensate the holders of those precarious titles.[a]

a. "Expropriation de N'Tabacoro: une arnaque à ciel ouvert," *L'Aube*, May 22, 2014.

---

obtaining a precarious or ownership title (Bertrand 1995, 2006; Leclerc-Olive and Keita 2004). Box 4.2 gives an example of the role of political and social connections in the public allocation of land.

Similarly, an ownership title will be granted all the more quickly and easily (even if the owner has left the property undeveloped) if additional sums have been paid to the various departments of the administration and the applicant is socially and politically well connected.

> The matter of corruption is brought up in all studies of land use management. All stakeholders consulted during various missions have mentioned it. Local elected councillors, customary landholders, prefecture officials, officials from the DRDC (Direction régionale des domaines et du cadastre, or Regional Directorate of State Domains and of the Land Register) and investors are all liable to benefit from corruption. It is important to recognize both its deep-rooted nature and its function in redistributing the profits anticipated by the various parties involved in the market, especially those who play a key role in the process of converting informal tenure rights into formal rights (Durand-Lasserve 2009, p. 16; translation from the original by the authors).

BOX 4.2

The Role of Political and Social Connections in the Public Allocation of Land: An Example

A list of households entitled to resettlement following a tenure regularization project that took place in a commune of Bamako District had been set up by the town council. People whose names were on the list had priority access to land in the resettlement area. A decision allocating a parcel of land for housing was made for the benefit of Mr. X, who had recently been evicted from his plot following a tenure regularization project. His name was on a list with many other beneficiary households. Less than a week later, another decision made by the same commune modified the list of beneficiaries. The land originally allocated to Mr. X was then reallocated to Mr. Y, a high-ranking ministerial officer. Officially, Mr. X had sold the land that had been allocated to him shortly after the allocation. The justification given by the land administration was that Mr. X sold his land either because he did not need it anymore or because he was unable to pay the administrative costs and fees associated with the allocation of the plot. Many other beneficiaries of the same resettlement scheme also "resold" their plots right after allocation. Mr. X may have been duped out of his plot, but he may also have been part of a concerted plan.

Source: Interview with a land administration official.

Suspicions of widespread corruption arise when reading the Auditor General's 2011 Annual Report (République du Mali 2012).[5]

The Legality of Sales

A plot may be sold by a holder of customary rights or an individual, usually with a certificate of sale, which should preferably be authenticated by the mayor's office (see annex 4A, which presents all the types of documents used for the different kinds of transaction) and is often known as a *"petit papier"* (bit of paper; see box 4.3). Although prohibited, this type of sale is very common. The authenticated certificate of sale is also often used to sell a plot with an administrative document or precarious title even though doing so is not legal. Many buyers are actually convinced that they have secure tenure because they have a document concerning the transaction that bears the signature of an authority.

To legally sell a plot with a precarious title (CR, CRUH, or CUH) requires a notarial deed or an equivalent act, and the authority that issued the precarious title must authorize the transfer of the land, confirming that it has indeed been developed; that charges, amounting to 7 percent of the price of the plot, have been paid; and that the lotissement where the plot is located is authorized. However, these conditions are rarely met.

BOX 4.3

Petits Papiers (Bits of Paper)

With regard to authenticated certificates of sale, Djiré and Traoré (2008, pp. 47–48) explain the misunderstandings they cause: "one of the limitations of *petits papiers* is that they commit only the signatory and only have effect if the latter acknowledges the commitments made, unless the buyer can demonstrate the authenticity of the signed document... . Generally speaking, buyers of land are less concerned with obtaining a document in the proper form that is unchallengeable in all respects than with simply having a document they could use against the seller or a third party with no such bit of paper. Consequently, they frequently opt for the least costly means of obtaining security of tenure. According to the notary,[a] most of the deeds concerning land transactions that he formalized, with the exception of those relating to ownership titles, were certifications of signature. Using this system, the buyer can escape the formalities of registration and related costs, but in so doing, denies himself the opportunity to give formal notice of the deed, which would give it legal effect vis-à-vis third parties." (translation from the original by the authors)

a. Interviewed by Djiré and Traoré.

Table 4.1 Degrees of Informality of Transactions on Land Markets According to the Type of Tenure and Documents Used in the Transaction

| Document used in the transaction | Tenure type | | | | |
| | | Precarious title · | | | |
	Ownership title	Transfer is authorized	Transfer is not authorized	Administrative document	No document
Notarial deed	Formal[a]	Formal[a]	Not possible	Not possible	Not possible
Authenticated certificate of sale	Not possible	Not authorized but tolerated (7)	Not authorized but common (6)	Not authorized but common (5)	Not authorized but common (4)
Nonauthenticated certificate of sale	Not possible	Transaction not authorized. Can be risky (3)	Transaction not authorized. Can be risky (2)	Transaction not authorized. Can be risky (2)	Transaction not authorized. Not common (1)

Note: The figure in brackets indicates the degree of informality of the transaction (1 for most informal, 7 for least informal).
a. Formal transaction provided the title delivery procedure is legal (see the section "Forced Ownership Titles and Multiple Allocation of a Lettre d' Attribution for the Same Plot" in this chapter).

Transactions that do not comply with legal rules are many. They are summarized in table 4.1, which takes into account both the type of tenure—formal or informal—of the transacted land and the legality of the transaction itself. Only transactions of ownership titles that have been the subject of a notarial deed are considered to be legal or formal. They require the payment of significant taxes and fees.

Land Delivery Channels and Market for Plots for Housing

Land markets feature different degrees of informality and formality (see chapter 2). Figure 4.2 shows the various degrees of formality on the land market. It also shows in which land delivery channel plots have been put onto the market for the very first time.

The Role of Stakeholders in the Land Delivery System

Stakeholders by Land Delivery Channel and Geographic Area
The land delivery system involves many stakeholders. Table 4.2 details their participation in the different land delivery channels and the geographic areas in which they operate. They have different functions that can be grouped into six main categories: (1) land suppliers and sellers; (2) land purchasers; (3) institutions governing land allocations and transactions (for example,

Figure 4.2 Land Markets for Plots for Housing According to the Degree of Formality

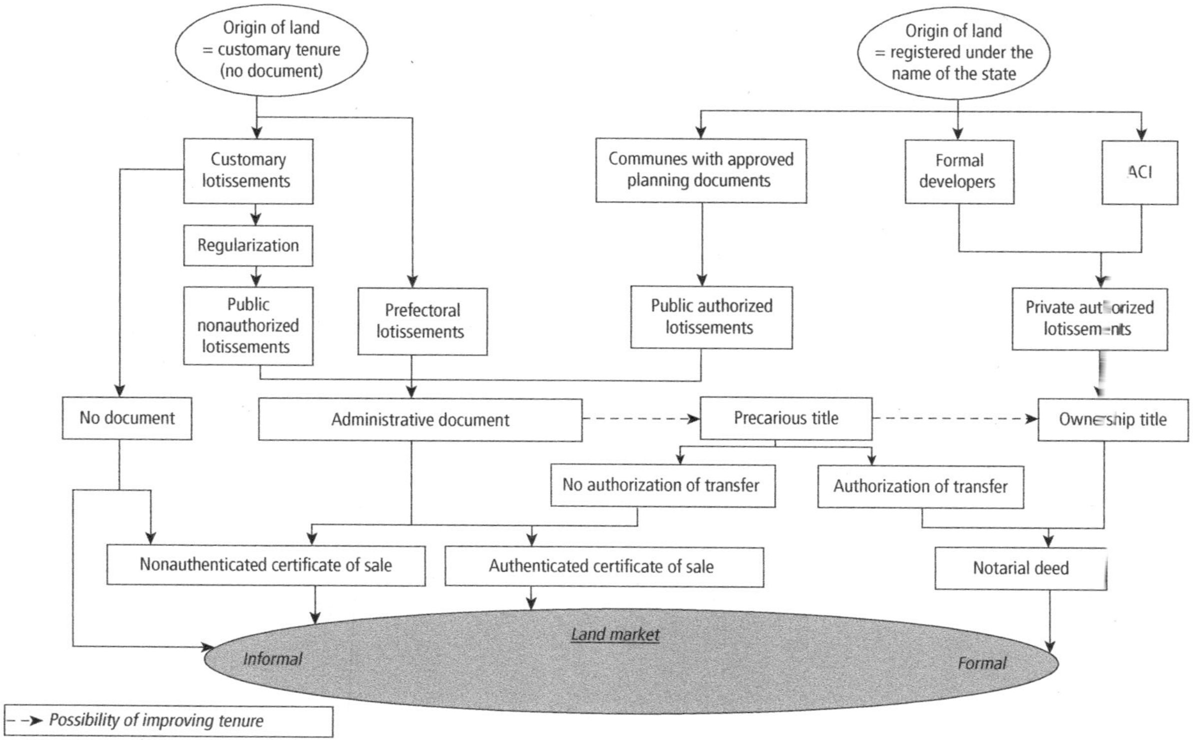

Table 4.2 Stakeholders Involved in Land Allocations and Transactions

Stakeholders		Land delivery channels			Main areas of involvement		
		Customary	Public and parapublic	Formal private	Bamako District	Bamako's peri-urban area	Bamako's rural hinterland
Land suppliers and sellers	Government institutions		*	*	*	*	*
	ACI		*		*	*	
	Communes (mayors)		*		*	*	*
	Individuals			*	*	*	*
	Customary landholders[a]	*				*	*
	Informal land developers	*				*	*
	Formal land developers		*	*	*	*	*
Land purchasers	Central and local government officers	*	*	*	*	*	*
	Merchants and traders	*	*		*	*	*
	Individuals	*	*	*	*	*	*
	Informal land developers and coxers	*	*			*	*
	Formal real estate developers	*	*	*	*	*	*
Institutions governing land allocations and transactions	Village authorities	*	*			*	*
	Peri-urban commune authorities (mayors)	*	*			*	
	Communes in Bamako District		*		*		
	Central government						
	Prefect; subprefect	*	*		*	*	*
	Council of Ministers	*	*	*	*	*	*
	DNDC DRDC (Koulikoro), and DDC-DB	*	*	*	*	*	*
	Cadastre and CARPOLE	*	*	*	*	*	*

(continued next page)

Table 4.2 (continued)

	Land delivery channels			Main areas of involvement		
Stakeholders	Customary	Public and parapublic	Formal private	Bamako District	Bamako's peri-urban area	Bamako's rural hinterland
Intermediaries						
Brokers	*	*	*	*	*	
Coxers	*	*	*	*	*	*
Professionals						
Land surveyors	*	*	*	*	*	*
Notaries		*	*	*	a	
Urban planners		*	*	*	*	
Credit and finance institutions		*	*	*	*	

Note: ACI = Agence de cession immobilière (Land Development Agency); DNDC = Direction nationale des domaines et du cadastre (National Directorate of State Domains and of the Land Register); DRDC = Direction régionale des domaines et du cadastre (Regional Directorate of State Domains and of the Land Register); CARPOLE = Cellule de Cartographie Polyvalente [Mapping Center]; DDC-DB : Direction des domaines et du cadastre du district de Bamako [Bamako District Directorate of State Domains and The Land Register]

a. When customary landholders do not sell customary land but land that has already been extracted from the customary channel, they are classified as "individuals."

providing authenticated certificates of sale, administrative documents, precarious titles, and ownership titles); (4) intermediaries between sellers, buyers, and authorities (brokers, coxers); (5) professionals (land surveyors who demarcate and subdivide land, notaries, and urban planners); and (6) credit and finance institutions.

The Services Provided by Some Stakeholders and Related Costs

Many of these stakeholders charge money for their services, which increases the cost of accessing land. Djiré (2006) highlights the very high official cost of the procedures required to obtain an ownership title on land sold by a customary holder in Sanankoroba rural commune.

In addition, the following information was obtained from informants: Institutions charge fees to authenticate a certificate of sale, authorize transfers, or issue titles. Some of these fees are statutory and others are illicit payments for which no receipt is given (see box 4.4).

Intermediaries also contribute to the cost of accessing land. In particular, coxers, who are looking for quick profits, play an important role. Taking advantage of sellers' trust and buyers' haste, they often try to secure maximum margins with little concern for the legality of the transactions. According to informants, a coxer may get a commission of between 5 percent and 10 percent of the price from the seller of customary land. The coxer may sometimes get a commission from the buyer as well. Coxers may help speed up the processing of applications for authenticated certificates of sale, or for precarious titles or ownership titles.

Finally, the remuneration of professionals is also a significant portion of the cost of accessing land. When the land is subdivided, land surveyors are paid

---

BOX 4.4

Costs of Services Provided by Some Stakeholders

According to informants for this study, 1 percent of the price of the land has to be paid to the mayor's office in Kati cercle to authenticate a certificate of sale for customary land. With that document, the land may be sold for double its purchase price. To move from an authenticated certificate of sale to a *concession rurale* (CR; rural concession), a buyer of rural land officially has to pay CFAF 60,000 per hectare, but the real cost of the transaction could be as much as CFAF 300,000 or even CFAF 400,000 per hectare. In all the communes, transferring precarious title requires authorization from the specialist bureau of the DRDC branch office in the commune that issued the title, costing 7 percent of the price of the land. The transfer may be refused if there is no notarial deed and if the land has not been developed. However, arrangements can be made to convince the administration.

in either plots or money. For the sale of customary land, they receive between 10 percent and 20 percent of the plots. Surveyors are not always officially authorized and sometimes act as both surveyor and coxer.

The Conflicts In the Land Delivery System

Land conflicts and disputes have long occupied an important place in Malian current affairs, but they have increased since 2010. Various associations of victims of evictions (from either urban or agricultural land) occupied the Labour Exchange in Bamako for three days in early April 2014. Conflicts, which may give rise to evictions and the destruction of housing, involve large numbers of people. They arise at the crossroads between the three channels and derive from (1) vagueness as to the scope and recognition of customary rights and the boundaries of the communes; (2) lotissement, regularization, and eviction and resettlement operations; and (3) the allocation of land with ownership title to Agence de cession immobilière (ACI, the Land Development Agency), property development companies, and housing cooperatives, together with the purchase by property development companies and housing cooperatives of customary land for which they have obtained ownership title (see chapter 3). The distinction between these three types of conflicts is somewhat theoretical because they can overlap. They most commonly arise when the surveyors arrive to carry out boundary marking and when houses are being demolished, usually with the support of police forces. The existence of several ownership titles or lettres d'attribution (see table 3.1) relating to the same piece of land causes large numbers of disputes that are either taken to court or settled by the interested parties themselves. According to the public prosecutor at the Supreme Court of Mali (République du Mali 2009), 80 percent of the many cases cluttering up the country's courts involve land tenure issues. The president of the bar affirms that tenure insecurity is the main cause of social conflict in Mali (République du Mali 2009).

Ill-Defined Customary Rights

Rules regarding the definition and enforcement of customary rights are imprecise. Inhabitants of villages holding customary rights often feel that they are being robbed. The *Code Domanial et Foncier* [2000 Land Code] establishes that, before registering or allocating land, the state must carry out a public inquiry with due hearing of all parties, but the relevant procedures have not been spelled out. This leads to conflicts that can involve holders of customary rights, the people to whom holders of customary rights have allocated or sold land, land and property development companies, the state, and communes. Examples are given in box 4.5.

BOX 4.5

Conflicts over Customary Rights

Customary landholders, land and property development companies, and occupants of customary land
The lotissement carried out by the SIFMA property development company in Sokonanfing village, Bamako commune III, was the subject of a petition for annulment filed in 2011 by the village's customary chiefs. SIFMA, however, argued that it had complied with all the rules. Its chief executive officer made the following statement: "A capital city cannot be managed under customary law when everyone knows that the land belongs to the state. The law establishes that, after *immatriculation* [registration of the land under the name of the state], the land can no longer revert to its earlier status."[a] This conflict, which was the subject of court proceedings, resulted in demolitions of houses and has had many repercussions.[b]

Customary landholders, communes, and occupants of land
In Dialakorodji commune, 3,000 people were chased off their plots and their houses were destroyed in 2004 at the request of the commune, although they insisted they had purchased these plots from the customary holders.[c]

In Mamaribougou-Dollarbougou (Mandé commune) houses built on plots forming part of a piece of land the mayor wished to subdivide were demolished. The plot occupants considered themselves to be expropriated because they have documents "signed by the village chief."[d]

a. "Litige foncier à Kouloumagni: le maire de la commune III accuse. La SIFMA dénonce une appropriation planifiée," *Mali Demain*, October 9, 2012.
b. "Haro sur les spéculateurs fonciers: Toutes les constructions illicites sur de titres fonciers d'autrui seront dorénavant démolies," *La Mutation*, May 6, 2014.
c. "Morcellement et occupation illicites de parcelles: les autorités municipales de Diala engagent la chasse aux sorcières contre les fautifs," *La Révélation*, April 27, 2011.
d. "Dollarbougou: l'affaire foncière qui divise," *Le Katois*, December 4, 2013.

It sometimes happens that, on the occasion of a resettlement in Bamako District, the youth of two neighborhoods fight over the customary rights of the land affected by the resettlement, arguing that their ancestors were the first to occupy the land. This is, for instance, the case of Sokonanfing and Koulouba neighborhoods.[6]

Lotissements, Regularization, and Eviction and Resettlement Operations

The conflicts presented above may derive from a lotissement operation, as happened in Dialakorodji commune (see box 4.5). Opposition from occupants of the land intended for the lotissement ended in one death, several injuries, and many arrests (Bourdarias 2003, 2006). The occupants of the land had previously been evicted from the adjacent neighborhood of Bamako commune I, which was involved in a lotissement in connection with a rehabilitation and regularization operation. This indicates that people are repeatedly displaced, always farther away from the city center.

The situation becomes very tense when the plots intended for resettlement are already occupied by people who have either previously purchased the land from or received it as a gift from holders of customary rights. Examples are given in box 4.6.

Allocations of Land with Ownership Title by the State to Communes, Property Development Companies, and Housing Cooperatives

Conflicts of interest between the state, Agence de cession immobilière (ACI; the Land Development Agency), and communes were numerous when the state allocated very large areas of land with ownership titles to ACI within the territory of Bamako communes, which had themselves launched lotissement

---

BOX 4.6

Lotissements, Regularization, and Resettlement Operations on Land Subject to Ownership Title

In the area of Missabougou neighborhood, in Bamako commune VI, the commune team granted many precarious titles on plots located on the property of a development company that had an ownership title. In June 2012, the governor of Bamako District ordered the mayor to stop the ongoing work on the site and annul the titles that had been granted.[a]

In February 2011, in Sebenikoro, Bamako commune IV, the resettlement of families on more than 260 lots, which had been carried out in 1996 by the town council and the governorate of Bamako District in connection with the Save Our Neighborhood program and the upgrading operation for the Sebenikoro settlement, was challenged by a company that said it was the owner of those lots.[b]

a. "Spéculation foncière à Missabougou: un seul coupable: le maire de la commune IV," *L'Indicateur du Renouveau*, October 18, 2012.
b. "Litige foncier à Sebénicoro: Plus de 260 familles menacées d'expropriation par la société GAMMA-SA," *L'Indépendant*, June 27, 2012.

operations although they had no ownership title (see "The Public and Parapublic Land Delivery Channel" section in chapter 3).

Since the early 2000s, land allocated by the state, either to certain communes in Kati cercle, which had a planning document approved by the Council of Ministers, or to property development companies—in particular to build social and affordable housing—or to housing cooperatives, has been subject to serious challenges from people who believe that they hold customary rights to that land and from people who have purchased plots from those customary holders and have built houses on it (Bertrand 2012).

An individual claiming to hold ownership title to a piece of land can threaten its occupants with eviction, as shown in box 4.7.

Expropriations in the Public Interest and Occupations of the State's Private Domain

Expropriations in the public interest typically occur in connection with infrastructure provision and give rise to conflicts exacerbated by delays in payment of compensation that may force some expropriated parties to sell their plots to speculators. According to a study on expropriations between 2010 and 2012 conducted by the *Groupe de suivi budgétaire* (a civil society organization), "The State would do well to compensate victims of land expropriation before implementing projects in the public interest in order to avoid land speculation by citizens."[7]

BOX 4.7

Disputes Concerning Ownership Titles

In Sénou-Plateau, Bamako commune VI, an individual attempted at the end of February 2012 to evict more than 2,000 families who had been settled for many years on land (with a total area of 60 hectares) affected by the Sénou infrastructure scheme drawn up by the council of commune VI. Claiming to hold ownership title, he had the 60 hectares surveyed and demarcated. The community mobilized against the plan; the police intervened and fired warning shots to disperse the demonstrators. Clashes lasted three days, resulting in injuries and arrests.[a] Following these incidents, the authorities[b] decided to chase that individual away and said they were prepared to conduct an inquiry to establish who was responsible.

a. "Situation explosive à Sénou: Babou Yara va exproprier plus de 2000 familles," *L'Indicateur du Renouveau*, February 29, 2012.
b. Ministries of Territorial Administration and Local Authorities, Housing, Land Affairs and Urban Planning, and the municipal and traditional authorities of Sénou.

Annex 4A Documents Used for Transactions (whether authorized or not)

Type of document	Documents that can be used and conditions
Purchase of customary land without subdivision	Certificate of sale, authenticated or not. Further transformation into precarious title and then ownership title possible.
Purchase of a plot following subdivision of customary land (plot with administrative documents: bulletins)	Authenticated certificate of sale and transfer of bulletin (bearing no name). Further transformation into precarious title (CRUH) possible and then ownership title possible
Purchase of a plot with an administrative document (lettre de notification or lettre d'attribution) issued by the commune	Authenticated certificate of sale. Sale by the beneficiary of the administrative document when he or she does not need the land, wants money immediately, or cannot pay the local development taxes. Common practice. Further possible transformation into precarious title (CUH).
Purchase of a plot with precarious title (CUH or CRUH)	Notarial deed if authorization of transfer granted by the commune that issued the concession. Authorization costs = 7 percent of the plot price. If taxes are paid, CUH or CRUH is issued in the buyer's name and possible further transformation into an ownership title if in an authorized lotissement.
	Or: authenticated certificate of sale. Transfers are often done without changing the holder's name to avoid paying authorization transfer.
Purchase of land or a plot with an ownership title. The purchase may concern all or part of the land with the ownership title: if just part, the buyer must obtain an ownership title for his or her individual plot.	Notarial deed of sale. Transfer charges amounting to 0.9 percent of the price.

Note: CRUH = concession rurale à usage d'habitation (rural concession for residential purposes); CUH = concession urbaine d'habitation (urban concession for residential purposes).

Notes

1. The term lotissement is often misused. According to Decree No. 05-115 of March 9, 2005 (which establishes the procedures for carrying out the different types of urban development operations), a lotissement is "the subdivision of a single piece of bare land into plots with appropriate provision of infrastructure and collective facilities to host the buildings to be erected by the future occupants." According to the decree, the lotissement requires the prior issuance of an ownership title, the approval of the regional director of urban planning and housing, and the authorization of the governor of the region or of the district for Bamako. Infrastructure and collective facilities are specified as "roads, drains/sewers, water supply, electricity and telephone." Field work conducted for this study showed that both residents and the authorities use the same word lotissement as a catchall term that refers to a wide range of land subdivisions. There are six types of lotissements (see chapter 3): (1) customary lotissements; (2) prefectoraux ones (both (1) and (2) are unauthorized, on land that is customary in origin); (3) lotissements by communes following a regularization

operation; these are authorized if the commune has an urban planning document approved by the state; (4) unauthorized commune lotissements; (5) private authorized lotissements; and (6) private unauthorized lotissements.

2. A person applying for precarious title (CUH or CRUH) must not have title to another plot in the same commune (apart from a joint plot), and any allocation of more than 1,000 square meters must be authorized by a state representative.

3. For example, in the area of Soro, he is said to have allocated several CRs covering 5 hectares each, a total area of 459 hectares, to a single person.

4. "Pour préserver des spéculations les sites mis à leur disposition à Gouana: Vers une union sacrée des deux plus grandes unions de coopératives d'habitat," *L'Indépendant*, March 20, 2014.

5. The report states (p. 55), "The DDC-DB [Direction des Domaines et du Cadastre du District de Bamako, or Bamako District Directorate of State Property and of the Land Register] reduced the sale prices of land, failing to apply the principle of uprating sale prices by a total amount of FCFA 80.35 million, in breach of the provisions of Decree No. 02-114/P-RM of March 6, 2002, establishing the sale prices and fees for urban and rural land in the State's private domain. In addition, the DDC-DB granted property developers who had not submitted approved property development programs unjustified facilities totalling FCFA 163.94 million in breach of the provisions of Decree No. N0-274/P-RM of June 23, 2000, setting out the procedures for granting facilities to property developers."

6. "Litiges fonciers : le courant ne passe plus entre Koulouba et Sokonanfing," *L'Indicateur du Renouveau*, April 26, 2013.

7. "Expropriation foncière par l'Etat entre 2010 et 2012: plus de 11,7 milliards de FCFA payés par le contribuable," *L'Indicateur du Renouveau*, February 13, 2014.

References

Bertrand, M. 1995. "Bamako, d'une République à l'autre." *Annales de la Recherche Urbaine* 66: 40–51.

———. 2006. "Foncier débridé/foncier bridé: enjeu récent de la décentralisation ou alternance centrale dans l'histoire longue des communes urbaines maliennes." In *Décentralisation des pouvoirs en Afrique en contrepoint des modèles territoriaux français*, edited by Claude Fay, 179–98. Paris: Institut de la recherche pour le développement.

———. 2012. "Du District au 'Grand Bamako' (Mali): Réserves foncières et tension, Gouvernance contestée." 13ème Conférence N-Aerus "la ville inégalitaire, espaces contestés, gouvernances en tension," Paris, November 22–24.

Bourdarias, F. 2003. "ONG et développement des élites." *Journal des Anthropologues* 94–95: 23–52.

———. 2006. "La décentralisation, la coutume et la loi: les constructions imaginaires d'un conflit à la périphérie de Bamako (Mali)." In *Décentralisation des pouvoirs en Afrique en contrepoint des modèles territoriaux français*, edited by Claude Fay, 221–38. Paris: Institut de la recherche pour le développement.

Djiré, M., and K. Traoré. 2008. "Assurer la sécurisation légale des transactions foncières: quel rôle pour les intermédiaires et facilitateurs?" Études de cas en zones péri-urbaine et dans le Mali-Sud, Support to the Legal Empowerment of the Poor, Legal Empowerment in Practice – LEP Working Paper, Food and Agriculture Organization of the United Nations.

Durand-Lasserve, A. 2009. "Harmonisation des systèmes fonciers au Mali par une inté-gration du droit coutumier au droit formel" Programme d'appui aux collectivités territoriales (Division Gestion du foncier communal), GTZ, Mali.

Leclerc-Olive, M., and A. Keita. 2004. "Les villes: laboratoires des démocraties?" Research report, PRUD (Programme de recherche urbaine pour le développement)/ISTED (Institut des sciences et des techniques de l'équipement et de l'environnement pour le développement)/GEMDEV (Groupement d'intérêt scientifique pour l'étude de la mondialisation et du développement), Paris.

République du Mali. 2009. "Actes de la rentrée judiciaire." Bulletin d'information de la Cour suprême du Mali, No. 10, Bamako.

———. 2012. "Bureau du Vérificateur général du Mali - Rapport 2011." Bamako.

Chapter 5

Results from a Survey of Land Transfers

Objective, Methodology, and Sample

Taking account of lessons learned from an analysis of the land delivery system and land markets (see figure 4.1), a survey was carried out between February and April 2012 to collect information on the features of transfers (public allocation, nonmonetary customary transfers and sales on the land market) of undeveloped (unbuilt) plots that occurred during the previous three years in the urban and peri-urban areas of Bamako and its rural hinterland (see table 2.1). The survey obtained information on 1,655 transfers that happened between 2009 and 2012 for undeveloped plots located between 3.5 and 72 kilometers away from the city center. Because the sample unit was the plot and not the household, information on each plot was collected by a team of investigators through a variety of local informants (neighbors, *coxers* [informal brokers], customary chiefs, buyers, users, sellers, and elected local officials). For each plot, the survey provides information on characteristics (land use, surface area, infrastructure, and services [water and electricity]), location (GPS coordinates, *commune* [administrative jurisdiction headed by a mayor], and distance to the closest paved road and to the river), tenure status (reported tenure types and corresponding documents), and price, as well as details on buyers and sellers. The questionnaire that was used is presented in annex 5A.

Although a strict random selection of plots was not possible, efforts were made to ensure uniform coverage of the survey zone, especially around roads extending outward from Bamako. In this sense, although the sample cannot be said to be perfectly representative of the universe of transferred plots in Bamako and its surrounding areas, conclusions may nevertheless be drawn about the characteristics of the major categories of transfers, shedding light on the options available to and the strategies of households to obtain land and try to obtain tenure security.

Map 2.1 shows the study area: the urban, peri-urban, and rural hinterland of Bamako, which extends over Bamako District, Kati *cercle* (administrative jurisdiction that includes several communes), and part of Koulikoro cercle. Information on transfers was collected within 27 communes in this zone.[1] Map 5.1 superimposes the plots in the sample on the same background. The shaded zone is the urbanized area as identified visually according to the criterion of density and contiguity of the built-up area. It extends beyond the boundaries of Bamako District. Beyond the shaded zone are the peri-urban areas and the rural hinterland.

Map 5.1 Locations of Plots in the Survey Sample

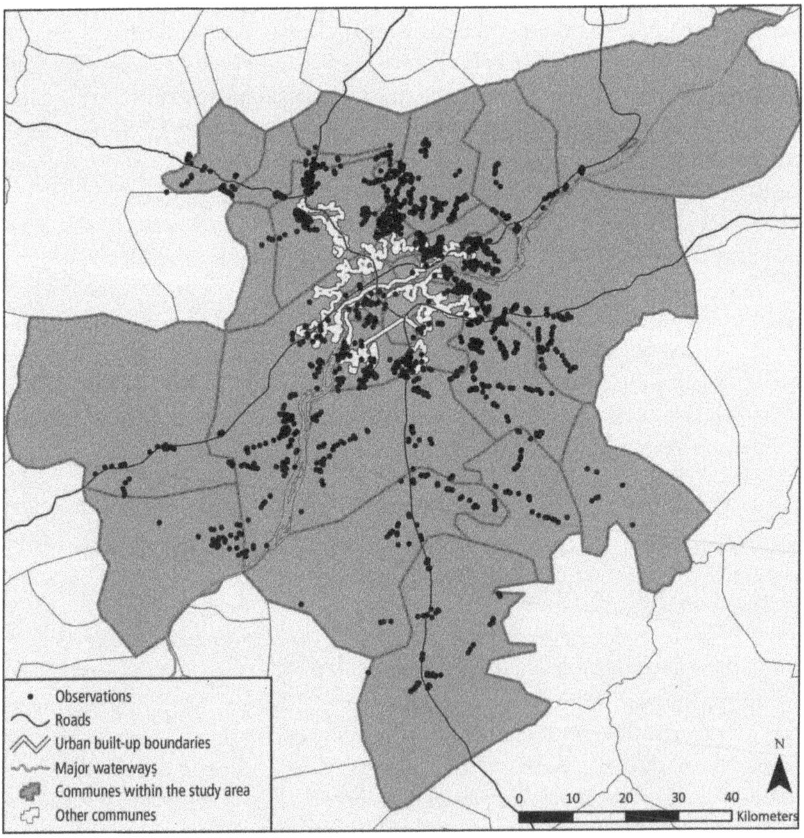

Source: Map prepared by Brian Blankespoor using data from the survey conducted in 2012 for the study and from Direction Nationale des Collectivités Territoriales.

The Spatial Segmentation of Land Transfers

The main purpose of the survey is to explore how land has been accessed in and around Bamako over a several-year period to identify modes of access to land as well as tenure and possible tenure transitions, accounting for the dynamic of the land delivery system (see figure 4.1). A period of only three years was chosen to ensure sufficient quality of responses to retrospective questions in this cross-sectional survey. According to the land delivery system described in chapter 4, transfers may be divided into four categories:

1. Purchase of land from a customary land holder and access to customary land without a monetary transaction
2. Allocation of a public land plot
3. Purchase of a land plot directly in a private formal *lotissement* (authorized subdivision of land made by a private developer)
4. Purchase of a land plot other than 1 and 3 on the land market.

To analyze the data collected, transfers are classified using the following categories:

- Purchase of land on the noncustomary land market, combining categories 3 and 4, which cannot be systematically distinguished using the collected data
- Public allocation of land (under which plots are obtained directly from a public authority), corresponding to category 2
- Purchase of land on customary market (plot transferred from a customary land holder by means of a monetary transaction), corresponding to a subcategory of category 1
- Nonmonetary customary access to land (customary land obtained in exchange for a symbolic payment of kola nuts, sometimes including a chicken as well), which corresponds to the other subcategory of category 1.

It should be noted that because the sample may not be perfectly representative of the universe of all transferred plots during the study period, it might not be representative of the relative sizes of the different categories of transfers, although it does give a rough idea. The objective of the survey is to illustrate the diversity of situations and means whereby households may access land and possibly improve the status of their tenure in Bamako and its surroundings. The sample is made up as follows: purchase of land on the noncustomary market (68 percent); public allocation of land (3 percent); purchase of land on the customary market (20 percent); and nonmonetary customary access to land (9 percent). It should be noted that these figures are indicative of the flows of recent land transfers involving undeveloped land and not of transfers making up the stock of developed or undeveloped plots in Bamako and the surrounding area.

The different types of transfers tend to occur in distinct areas as shown in figure 5.1, which plots the geographic coordinates of the sample's plots by transfer category.

Types of transfers vary from place to place. Although those involving public land and the noncustomary market are spread throughout the study area, they occupy relatively central locations. In contrast, monetary transactions and nonmonetary transfers of customary land occur in the outer rings of the peri-urban area and rural hinterland. The database reveals a not inconsiderable number of nonmonetary transfers involving customary land located on the outer fringes: whereas the median monetary customary transaction occurs 32 kilometers away from the city center, the median nonmonetary transfer is 37 kilometers away. These findings corroborate previous observations made by social scientists on the "emergence of land markets" fueled by urban expansion and the conversion of customary land in peri-urban areas in Africa (Durand-Lasserve 2004; Rakodi and Leduka 2004; Wehrmann 2008).

Figure 5.1 Spatial Patterns of Land Transfers

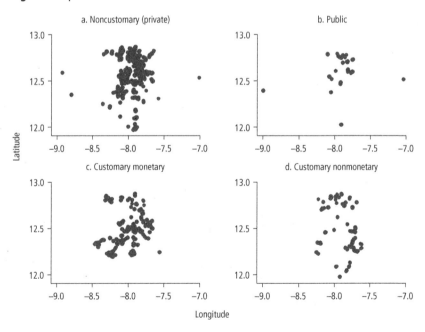

Source: Survey conducted in 2012 for this study.

The basic characteristics of different types of transfers are further detailed in table 5.1. It can be seen that plots transferred according to custom by a customary owner are primarily for agricultural use (83 precent), whereas almost half of the transactions on the customary market were intended for residential use at the time of the survey. This illustrates the conversion of customary land into urban land following monetary transactions and the competition between the two uses in areas where the land market is developing under the influence of the city. As expected though, residential plots (which account for more than two-thirds of the sample) are closer to the city center than agricultural land. This is the case in the whole sample as well as within each transfer category.

The median price of plots at the time of the transfer is higher for transactions on the noncustomary market than for monetary customary transactions, which seems logical given that the plots sold on the noncustomary market are closer to the city center (figure 5.1) and that the process of formalization is further advanced there.[2]

Table 5.2 presents the profile of sellers and buyers by transfer category. Most sellers of plots are farmers (63 percent) but their share is considerably higher in nonmonetary customary transfers (97 percent) than in the customary market (84 percent) and on the noncustomary market (56 percent, but 53 percent for residential plots and 73 percent for agricultural plots). It is interesting to note that the share of coxers identified as sellers of plots is highest on the noncustomary market (16 percent).[3]

In contrast to their activity as sellers, farmers form only a small minority (12 percent) of buyers of plots. Although the occupation of an important proportion of buyers is not known, the figures suggest that buyers' characteristics depend on the type of transfer. While farmers represent 77 percent of those who access land through a nonmonetary transfer of customary plots, they represent only 9 percent of buyers on the customary land market, and 4 percent of buyers on the noncustomary land market. Note that farmers demanding land in the land markets are likely to be investors purchasing land, whereas farmers demanding land through the nonmonetary customary land access mode are most probably low-income households likely to have been granted a right to use the land rather than "ownership" of the plot. The small proportion of farmers buying land on the noncustomary land market reflects the essentially residential nature of this market (table 5.1).

The survey also highlights women's weak involvement in land transfers. Regarding residential land, women represent only 18 percent of buyers in the noncustomary market, 15 percent of beneficiaries of public land allocation, 13 percent of buyers in the customary market, and 8 percent of those who received customary land according to custom. This seems to indicate that women have very little access to land through customary channels and only marginally more via public transfers and the noncustomary market. The figures

Table 5.1 Characteristics of Land Transfers

Type of transfer	Definition	Number of observations	Median distance to city center (kilometers)	Proportion of plots intended for residential use (percent)	Median size		Median price (at time of transfer)	
					Residential (square meters)	Agricultural (hectares)	Residential (CFA francs per square meter)	Agricultural (CFA francs per hectare)
Noncustomary market	Land bought from noncustomary land holder (including previously allocated public land and previously customary land)	1,120	21	84	300	2	1,125	500,000
Public	Land directly allocated by central or local government	52	21	75	300	2	1,583	750,000
Customary market	Customary land bought from customary landholder	328	32	47	400	3	823	300,000
Customary nonmonetary	Land obtained through customary mechanism	154	37	17	450	2	n.a.	n.a.

Source: Survey conducted in 2012 for this study.
Note: n.a. = not applicable.

Table 5.2 Buyers and Sellers (or Providers) of Land According to Type of
Transfer and Occupation
percent

Occupation	Type of transfer							
	Noncustomary market		Public		Customary market		Customary nonmonetary	
	Sellers	Buyers	Sellers	Buyers	Sellers	Buyers	Sellers	Buyers
Farmer	56	4	0	4	84	9	97	77
Private sector activity	13	43	0	38	5	41	0	14
Public sector activity	14	26	94	27	1	31	2	6
Coxer	16	1	0	2	4	2	1	0
Unknown	1	26	6	29	5	17	0	3
Total	100	100	100	100	100	100	100	100

Source: Survey conducted in 2012 for this study.

are even lower for agricultural land, where women represent between 5 percent
and 6 percent of buyers depending on the type of transfer.

Another interesting result relates to the place of residence of buyers: more
than 60 percent of customary and noncustomary transactions, and public
transfers of plots located outside Bamako District are undertaken by individuals
who actually live in Bamako District. Some 70 percent of these plots are for residential use, but only 25 percent of them have been developed since the date of
the transaction, which is suggestive of an important proportion of speculative
holdings. Very few buyers involved in nonmonetary customary transfers live in
Bamako District; 72 percent of them actually reside in the commune where land
was bought, which is consistent with local small farmers being granted the right
to use the land under a symbolic exchange. As for Malian expatriates, they are
mostly purchasing land on the noncustomary land market, where they represent 7 percent of all buyers.

Land Tenure Patterns at the Time of the Transfer

Focusing on tenure at the time of transfer, table 5.3 ("All plots" column) shows
that the majority of plots (53 percent) were held at the time of transfer with
some administrative document (*bulletin, lettre de convocation, lettre de notification*, or *lettre d'attribution*; see table 3.1 for definitions of these documents and
the context in which they can be obtained).[4] These administrative documents
are usually issued in connection with a regularization operation (see
"Administrative Allocation of Residential Plots in Authorized Lotissements and

Table 5.3 Tenure Status at Time of Transfer by Intended Use of Plot
percent

Tenure status	All plots (1,655 observations)[a]	Residential plots (1,104 observations)	Agricultural plots (463 observations)
No administrative document	29.1	16.1	60.0
Administrative document	53.0	62.5	30.2
Precarious title	12.7	15.6	7.6
Ownership title	5.0	5.7	2.2
Unknown	0.1	0.1	0.0
Total	100	100	100

Source: Survey conducted in 2012 for this study.
a. This number includes 88 observations for which the information on plot use is missing.

Lotissements with Regularization" in chapter 3) and provide entitlement to apply for a precarious title. Only 13 percent of plots had a precarious title. Only 5 percent of the plots in the survey were held with an ownership title at the time of transfer. About 29 percent of the plots were transferred without any administrative documentation.

In addition, the majority of plots for residential use (which represent more than two-thirds of the sample) are often held with an administrative document (62 percent). The proportion of plots held with no administrative documentation is only 16 percent, while the proportion of plots held with a precarious title (occupancy permit or *concessions à usage d'habitation* [urban and rural concessions for residential purposes]) or an ownership title totals 21 percent (approximately 15 percent and 6 percent, respectively).

The lack of documentation is more pronounced for plots for agricultural use (which represent less than one-third of the sample). At the time of transfer, only 10 percent of them were held with a precarious or ownership title (8 percent and 2 percent, respectively). Some 30 percent of agricultural plots have an administrative document, and 60 percent have no administrative document at all.[5]

When looking simultaneously at the type of transfer and tenure status at the time of transfer for all the plots (table 5.4), it can be seen that a majority of plots obtained on the noncustomary market have an administrative document (51 percent) that is issued only by the public authorities (communes and prefects) and that is designed in principle to regularize occupants' situations.[6] Only 3 percent of the sample's plots are directly obtained by public transfer. It may therefore be assumed that a large number of holders of regularized plots do not keep their plots but sell them on the noncustomary informal market (figure 4.2). Only 16 percent of the sample's plots are obtained on the noncustomary market with a title (12 percent with a precarious title and 4 percent with an ownership title). Some 29 percent of transfers are customary (monetary and according to custom), and all involve plots without any administrative document. This shows that customary channels and the noncustomary informal market play a key role in land supply and

Table 5.4 Tenure Status and Type of Transfers at Time of Transfer
percent

Tenure status	Type of transfer				
	Noncustomary market	Public	Customary market	Customary nonmonetary	Total
No administrative document	0.0	0.0	19.8	9.3	29.1
Administrative document	51.4	1.6	0.0	0.0	53.0
Precarious title	11.8	1.0	0.0	0.0	12.7
Ownership title	4.4	0.6	0.0	0.0	5.0
Unknown	0.1	0.0	0.0	0.0	0.1
Total	67.7	3.1	19.8	9.3	100

Source: Survey conducted in 2012 for this study.

Table 5.5 Median Distance to City Center by Tenure Status at Time of Transfer
kilometers

Tenure status	Median distance to city center		
	All plots	Residential plots	Agricultural plots
No administrative document	33	23	38
Administrative document	22	21	29
Precarious title	18	17	21
Ownership title	16	13	23

Source: Survey conducted in 2012 for this study.

have taken over from direct allocation of public land, the supply of which appears to be exhausted or frozen during the studied period. Some 16 percent of transfers took place on the noncustomary market for plots with a title (12 percent with precarious title and 4 percent with ownership title), which suggests that tenure formalization processes are more advanced for plots sold on the noncustomary market than for plots sold on the customary market.

The different tenure situations exhibit noticeable spatial patterns that partly reflect the spatial stratification of different types of transfers. As can be seen from table 5.5, more-secure and more-formal tenure situations are located closer to the center of Bamako: the median distance from the city center for plots with ownership titles in the sample is 16 kilometers whereas it is 33 kilometers for plots without administrative documents. Intermediate forms of tenure (administrative documents and precarious titles) occupy intermediate locations in the city. This is true for the sample as a whole but also within the subsamples of residential and agricultural plots. A series of both economic and historic elements could explain the location of the most formal tenure, which is, on average, closer to the city center.[7] One explanation could be that richer individuals who have the financial means and social networks to formalize tenure prefer to reside closer to the city. Another explanation is that there are higher incentives to hold formal documents for land close to the city center: because proximity to the city center commands greater land values, occupants who do not have formal titles are exposed to a higher risk of conflict and evictions as a result of market pressures. A third explanation could be that formal lotissements where plots are sold with ownership titles are located close to the city center, mechanically increasing the proportion of plots held under formal tenure in central locations. Finally, plots closer to the city center were converted to residential use earlier, and successive regularizations have taken place over time and ever farther away from the city center.

Of course, there is not a complete spatial stratification of tenure, and various tenure situations may be observed in a given area. Figure 5.2 represents the land tenure mix at the time of the survey for different distance ranges from the center of Bamako. Farther away from the city center, the share of more formal types of tenure (precarious titles and ownership titles) diminishes in favor of less secure tenure types (administrative documents at best). Figure 5.2 thus illustrates the phasing out

Figure 5.2 Tenure by Distance to the City Center

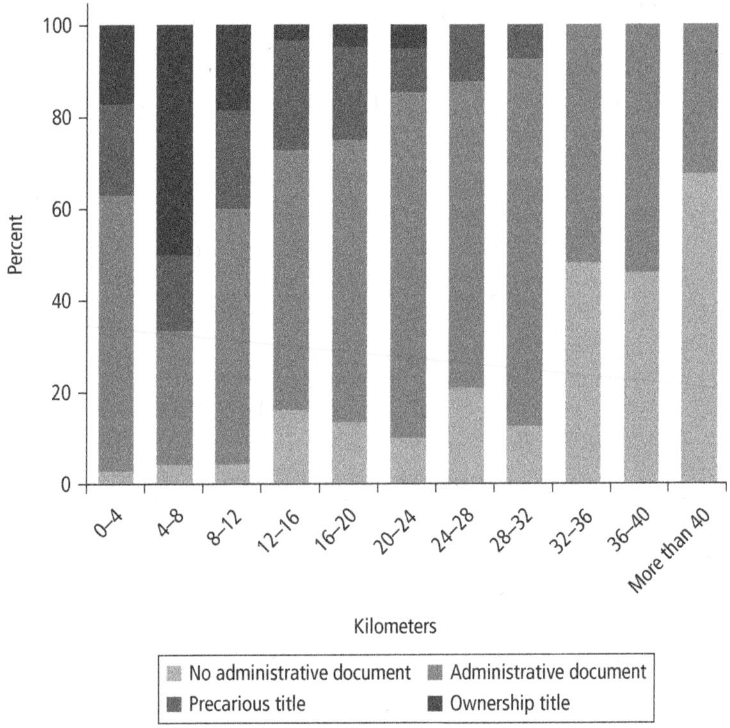

Source: Survey conducted in 2012 for this study.

of formality as distance from the city center increases: there are no ownership titles in the sample more than 24 kilometers away from Bamako and no precarious titles farther than 32 kilometers. The proportion of plots held under administrative documents decreases to about one-third 40 kilometers and more away from Bamako.

Land Tenure Conversions

Another result from the survey is that tenure might evolve between the date of the transfer and the date of the survey (over a period of at most three years). Table 5.6 presents the tenure transitions for the entire sample since the date of the transfer.[8] The tenure of about 25 percent of the plots in the survey was reported to have changed since they were transferred. Most transitions occurred at the bottom and middle of the tenure typology. Among the plots that experienced land tenure conversion, 45 percent were granted an administrative document, 47 percent a precarious title, and 8 percent an ownership title.

The type of observed transition varies depending on the type of transfer (calculations not reflected in the table). For instance, 91 percent of customary plots that were transferred with no money changing hands remained customary (the nature of the transfer is likely to involve the provision of a customary "right" to use the plot as agricultural land). The figure drops to 22 percent for customary plots that were purchased. Who holds the plot also seems to matter—civil servants and merchants seem to have had an advantage in the purchase and tenure transformation of plots. About 35 percent of those obtaining a precarious title on initially customary land were civil servants. About 42 percent of those obtaining a precarious title on initially

Table 5.6 Tenure Transition Matrix: All Plots
percent

Tenure at time of survey / Tenure at time of transfer	No administrative document	Administrative document	Precarious title	Ownership title	Unknown	Total
No administrative document	13.4	11.1	3.5	0.7	0.4	29.1
Administrative document	0.0	44.4	8.0	0.5	0.0	53.0
Precarious title	0.0	0.0	12.0	0.7	0.1	12.7
Ownership title	0.0	0.0	0.0	5.0	0.0	5.0
Unknown	0.0	0.0	0.0	0.0	0.1	0.1
Total	13.4	55.5	23.5	7.0	0.5	100.0

Source: Survey conducted in 2012 for this study.

Table 5.7 Tenure Transition Matrix: Residential Plots
percent

Tenure at time of survey						
Tenure at time of transfer	No administrative document	Administrative document	Precarious title	Ownership title	Unknown	Total
No administrative document	7.6	7.0	1.0	0.2	0.4	16.1
Administrative document	0.0	54.0	8.1	0.5	0.0	62.5
Precarious title	0.0	0.0	14.9	0.5	0.1	15.6
Ownership title	0.0	0.0	0.0	5.7	0.0	5.7
Unknown	0.0	0.0	0.0	0.0	0.1	0.1
Total	7.6	61.0	24.0	6.9	0.5	100.0

Source: Survey conducted in 2012 for this study.

customary land were merchants (and 25 percent were civil servants or military personnel).

Table 5.7 represents tenure transitions for the subsample of plots destined for residential use. Observed conversions are very similar to those for the sample as a whole and confirm that the process of tenure improvement does not continue through to the end but very frequently stopped before an ownership title is obtained.[9]

Changes in tenure do not seem to be concentrated in any particular areas.

Land Tenure and Land Prices

The data collected on transaction and public allocation prices (both at the time of transfer and at the time of the survey) allow the determinants of land prices in Bamako to be studied. The main objective is to measure the contribution of tenure and spatial location to price differences in an effort to assess the values of both the different land tenure situations and the prevailing spatial patterns. In theory, land prices are expected to be related to physical characteristics such as plot size, location (physical accessibility to the city center), and availability of services (water or electricity), as well as to tenure status (security and rights, such as transferability, associated with each type of tenure). Hedonic price analysis is used to investigate how prices are correlated with tenure and location, controlling for other characteristics. This is done for all plot transfers with a "price," thus excluding from the pooled sample of observations the plots obtained through the nonmonetary customary mode and treating public allocations as if they were occurring on a land market.[10] To address possible outlier issues, observations for which the price of land per square meter was in the top or bottom 1 percent of the price distribution were removed. The estimated equation is of the form

$$\text{Log}(p_i) = \alpha d_i + \beta t_i + \gamma d_i \times t_i + \sum_j w_j X_i^j + \varepsilon_i.$$

In this equation p_i is the price per square meter of plot i (which can be either the price paid at the date of the transfer or the estimated price at the date of the survey), t_i is a set of dummy variables describing the tenure on the land, d_i is the Euclidean distance to the city center. X_i^j is a vector of the various covariates j present in the database, such as the distance to the nearest paved road, the area of the plot, whether the land is serviced (water, electricity, or both), and the riverbank on which the land is located. The area of the plot is included (even though the dependent variable is price per square meter) in order to capture nonlinear effects.

The coefficients of the regression are estimated by ordinary least squares.[11] Results are presented in table 5.8 for four different specifications. Specifications (1) and (2) use the price at the time of transfer as the explained variable whereas

Table 5.8 Land Price Regressions, All Uses

	Regression using transfer price		Regression using estimated price at time of survey	
	(1)	(2)	(3)	(4)
Dummy: Agricultural use	−0.422***	−0.400***	−0.476***	−0.458***
	(0.101)	(0.101)	(0.096)	(0.095)
Distance to city center (kilometers)	−0.069***	−0.068***	−0.068***	−0.101***
	(0.004)	(0.007)	(0.004)	(0.012)
Dummy: Administrative document	0.071	−0.052	−0.034	−1.054***
	(0.066)	(0.199)	(0.087)	(0.304)
Dummy: Precarious title	0.672***	1.458***	0.215**	−0.124
	(0.085)	(0.256)	(0.093)	(0.319)
Dummy: Ownership title	1.912***	1.842***	1.346***	0.880**
	(0.127)	(0.331)	(0.121)	(0.351)
Distance × administrative document		0.006		0.045***
		(0.008)		(0.013)
Distance × precarious title		−0.044***		0.011
		(0.012)		(0.013)
Distance × ownership title		0.005		0.017
		(0.018)		(0.016)

(continued next page)

Table 5.8 (continued)

	Regression using transfer price		Regression using estimated price at time of survey	
	(1)	(2)	(3)	(4)
Area of the plot (in log)	−0.422***	−0.428***	−0.423***	−0.421***
	(0.026)	(0.026)	(0.024)	(0.024)
Dummy: South bank of the river	0.793***	0.782***	0.742***	0.722
	(0.50)	(0.050)	(0.046)	(0.046)
Distance to paved road (kilometers)	−0.077***	−0.077***	−0.086***	−0.084***
	(0.005)	(0.005)	(0.005)	(0.004)
Access to water	0.662***	0.649***	0.762***	0.707***
	(0.139)	(0.139)	(0.134)	(0.134)
Access to electricity	0.092	0.165	−0.050	−0.014
	(0.310)	(0.308)	(0.303)	(0.300)
Dummy: Sold in 2010	0.210***	0.199***		
	(0.062)	(0.062)		
Dummy: Sold in 2011	0.282***	0.282***		
	(0.063)	(0.062)		
Dummy: Sold in 2012	0.295***	0.290***		
	(0.103)	(0.103)		
Number of observations	1,239	1,239	1,289	1,289
R²	0.79	0.79	0.79	0.80

Note: Ordinary least squares regressions for pooled residential and agricultural plots, excluding 1 percent of highest and lowest prices. In models (1) and (2), the tenure dummies are at transfer time. In models (3) and (4), the tenure dummies are at the time of the survey. Constant not shown.
*** denotes significance at the 1 percent level, ** at the 5 percent level, and * at the 10 percent level.

specifications (3) and (4) use the estimated price at the time of the survey.[12] Specifications (1) and (3) exclude the interaction term between distance and tenure category whereas specifications (2) and (4) include it. Inclusion of this term can account for different price gradients depending on the tenure category. All specifications include a dummy for plots that are destined for agricultural use (as opposed to residential).

Results are consistent across the different specifications. The land market in Bamako displays the patterns that could be expected from any land market: prices decrease with distance from the city center and road infrastructure, and increase for serviced plots. Residential plots are more highly valued than agricultural plots. Plots with precarious or ownership title are, on average, more expensive than plots with less secure forms of tenure. Except for regression (4), the price of plots with only administrative documents does not differ significantly from those without any documents, which suggests that an administrative document is not very valuable.[13] Across specifications, plots with ownership titles are worth 1.4 to 5.7 times the price of similar plots with no legal rights, demonstrating the high value of tenure formality and security as well as of transferability.

To allow for the possibility that characteristics are priced differently depending on the agricultural or residential use of plots, the same regressions are run for the subsample of residential plots. The results presented in table 5.9 are qualitatively and quantitatively very similar to those presented in table 5.8.

Regressions (1) and (2) in table 5.9, which use prices at the date of transfer, make it possible to come up with a rough estimate of the annual rate of increase in land prices for plots destined for residential use. It is important to note that

Table 5.9 Land Price Regression, Residential Use

	Regression using transfer price		Regression using estimated price at time of survey	
	(1)	(2)	(3)	(4)
Distance to city center (kilometers)	−0.072***	−0.055***	−0.068***	−0.105***
	(0.004)	(0.10)	(0.004)	(0.015)
Dummy: Administrative document	−0.038	0.213	−0.178**	−1.205***
	(0.079)	(0.241)	(0.094)	(0.338)
Dummy: Precarious title	0.598***	1.840***	0.139	0.044
	(0.098)	(0.297)	(0.101)	(0.363)
Dummy: Ownership title	1.727***	2.087***	1.295***	0.507
	(0.138)	(0.348)	(0.130)	(0.383)
Distance × administrative document		−0.011		0.049***
		(0.011)		(0.016)
Distance × precarious title		−0.070***		−0.003
		(0.015)		(0.018)
Distance × ownership title		−0.017		0.038**
		(0.020)		(0.020)
Area of the plot (in log)	−0.445***	−0.459***	−0.419***	−0.425***
	(0.036)	(0.035)	(0.033)	(0.032)
Dummy: South bank of the river	0.794***	0.787***	0.823***	0.799***
	(0.056)	(0.057)	(0.050)	(0.051)
Distance to paved road (kilometers)	−0.074***	−0.075***	−0.078***	−0.077***
	(0.006)	(0.006)	(0.005)	(0.005)
Access to water	0.587***	0.608***	0.655***	0.612***
	(0.152)	(0.150)	(0.141)	(0.140)
Access to electricity	0.135	0.153	0.059	0.017
	(0.362)	(0.361)	(0.338)	(0.335)

(continued next page)

Table 5.9 (continued)

	Regression using transfer price		Regression using estimated price at time of survey	
	(1)	(2)	(3)	(4)
Dummy: Sold in 2010	0.265***	0.235***		
	(0.071)	(0.071)		
Dummy: Sold in 2011	0.297***	0.289***		
	(0.069)	(0.069)		
Dummy: Sold in 2012	0.406***	0.381***		
	(0.112)	(0.112)		
Number of observations	991	991	1,016	1,016
R^2	0.63	0.64	0.64	0.65

Note: Ordinary least squares regressions for residential plots only, excluding 1 percent of highest and lowest prices. In models (1) and (2), the tenure dummies are at transfer time. In models (3) and (4), the tenure dummies are at the time of the survey. Constant not shown.
*** denotes significance at the 1 percent level, ** at the 5 percent level, and * at the 10 percent level.

with these data, such estimates can only be very rough and may possibly provide an underestimation of land price increases; for instance, buyers and sellers may tend to underreport the price they agreed on (for fear of taxes or to avoid pressure from relatives or people who may have a claim on the same plot), thus biasing downward the amount paid for recent land transfers.[14] According to the data, prices are found to have increased by about 40 percent during the period covered by the study, which would indicate an increase of about 16 percent per year.[15] Restricting the sample to plots with ownership titles yields an annual price increase estimate of about 20 percent. Bearing in mind the imperfections in the data, the results point to land price increases that were much higher than the nominal growth in GDP per capita (2.6 percent in 2010 and 0.35 percent in 2011) and in the range of 10 times the official inflation rate (the consumer price index has increased by 2 percent annually between 2008 and 2011). Given the high ratio of land prices to household incomes, this is indicative of a significant decrease in affordability.

An important result of the analysis is to show the negative land price gradient for Bamako. This is illustrated below for residential plots only and for prices at the time of transfer by estimating a hedonic price regression with the same explanatory variables as in specification (1) in table 5.9 but excluding the distance variable. Residuals from this estimation are then plotted against distance from the city center and presented in figure 5.3. The figure provides a simple graphical representation of the contribution to price of proximity to the city center, excluding the effects of the other variables. The negative gradient confirms the higher value of land close to the city center and the influence of Bamako throughout the study area.

Figure 5.3 Land Price Gradient, Residential Use

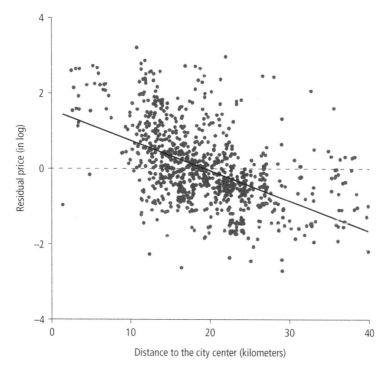

Annex 5A Questionnaire

STUDY ON LAND ACCESS COSTS IN THE URBAN AND PERI-URBAN AREAS OF
BAMAKO AND IN ITS RURAL HINTERLAND

PLOT LEVEL SURVEY

THE SURVEY COVERS ONLY PLOTS OF LAND THAT WERE TRANSFERRED AFTER JANUARY 1, 2009

IDENTIFICATION

AREA TYPE: ☐ 1. Urban ☐ 2. Peri-urban ☐ 3. Rural hinterland	DATE OF SURVEY:
COMMUNE: _____	DAY: /_/_/
NEIGHBORHOOD: _____	MONTH: /_/_/
SECTOR: _____	YEAR: /_/_/_/
VILLAGE: _____	INITIALS OF ENUM.: /_/_/
AREA OF PLOT ACCORDING TO SOURCE: _____	MAIN INFORMANT(S) / SOURCE(S) (MULTIPLE ANSWERS POSSIBLE):
UNIT: ☐ 1. Hectares ☐ 2. Ares ☐ 3. Square meters	
	☐ 1. Resident of neighborhood/village
AREA OF PLOT ACCORDING TO ENUMERATOR: _____	☐ 2. Customary chief / head of the village
UNIT: ☐ 1. Hectares ☐ 2. Ares ☐ 3. Square meters	☐ 3. Coxer, informant or other intermediary
LATITUDE OF PLOT: N /_/_/ /_/_/_/_/_/	☐ 4. Buyer or allottee residing on plot
LONGITUDE OF PLOT: W /_/_/ /_/_/_/_/_/	☐ 5. Buyer or allottee not residing on plot
USE AT TIME OF SURVEY: ☐ 1. Plot for residential use	☐ 6. Resident on plot (other than buyer or allottee)
☐ 2. Plot for agricultural use	☐ 7. Seller of plot
☐ 3. Other	☐ 8. Mayor or elected commune official
DISTANCE TO PAVED ROAD: _____	☐ 9. Government technical services
UNIT: ☐ 1. Kilometers ☐ 2. Meters	☐ 10. Other (specify):
DISTANCE TO RIVER: ☐ 1. 100 meters or less	_____
☐ 2. More than 100 meters and less than 500	
☐ 3. 500 meters and more	

ENUMERATOR'S COMMENTS (TO BE FILLED IN AT THE END OF INTERVIEW): _____ _____ _____	

REMARK: THE SURVEY COVERS PLOTS THAT HAVE BEEN TRANSACTED, DONATED, OR ALLOCATED

DATE OF TRANSFER (PURCHASE, DONATION, OR ALLOCATION)

	Question	Categories	Answer
Q01	When was the plot purchased, donated, or allocated?	Months: 1 to 12 Years: 09, 10, 11 or 12 99. Does not know	Month /_/_/ Year /_/_/

TRANSFER (PURCHASE/DONATION/ALLOCATION) OF PLOT

	Question	Categories	Answer
Q02	Who purchased/received/obtained the plot?	1. Man 2. Woman 3. Man and woman jointly 4. Other members of the same family 5. Association or cooperative 6. Private company 7. Public institution 8. Other(s). Specify: _____ 9. Does not know	/_/
Q03	Was the plot obtained through a resettlement project?	1. Yes 2. No 9. Does not know	/_/

Q04	What is the occupation/status of the person who purchased/received/obtained the plot?	10. Farmer
		20. Merchant/trader
		30. Private sector employee
		40. Professional
		50. Land property developer/informal developer/coxer
		60. Public administration employee
		  61. At central government level
		  62. At local authority level
		70. Members of security and defense services
		80. Elected official, political leader
		  81. At national level
		  82. At local level
		90. Other/No occupation. Specify: _____
		99. Does not know
			/_/_/

Q05	Where does the person who purchased/received/obtained the plot reside?	10. In the same *commune*
		  11. On the plot covered by this survey
		  12. On another plot
		20. In another *commune* of Bamako District
		30. In another *commune* of Kati *cercle*
		40. In another town or region of Mali
		50. Abroad
		60. Other. Specify: _____
		99. Does not know
			/_/_/

TRANSFER (SALE/DONATION/ALLOCATION) OF PLOT

	Question	Categories	Answer

Q06	The plot was sold/donated/allocated by...	10. An individual
		  11. Customary "owner"
		  12. Non customary/statutory owner
		20. Housing developer or land developer (formal sector)
		  21. Parastatal agency (ACI)\\
		  22. Housing or land developer from the private sector
		30. State/central government
		  31. Governor
		  32. Prefect
		  33. Subprefect
		  34. Council of Ministers
		40. Commune
		  41. Through a resettlement project
		  42. In a land development project (other than resettlement)
		50. Other. Specify: _____
		99. Does not know
			/_/_/

Q07	The person who sold/donated/ the plot was…	1. Man 2. Woman 3. Man and woman jointly 4. Others members of a same family 9. Does not know	/_/

Q08	At the time of transfer, what was the occupation/status of the person who sold/donated/ the plot?	10. Farmer
		20. Merchant/Trader
		30. Private sector employee
		40. Professional
		50. Land property developer/informal developer/coxer
		60. Public administration employee
		    61 At central government level
		    62 At local authority level
		70. Members of security and defense services
		80. Elected official, political leader
		    81. At national level
		    82. At local level
		90. Other/No occupation. Specify: _____
		99. Does not know
			/_/_/

Q09	At the time of transfer, where did the person who sold/donated/transferred the plot reside?	1. In the same *commune* 2. In another *commune* of Bamako District 3. In another *commune* of Kati *cercle* 4. In another town or region of Mali 5. Abroad 6. Other. Specify: _____ 9. Does not know	/_/
Q10	Did the person who sold/donated the plot receive it through a resettlement project?	1. Yes 2. No 9. Does not know	/_/

DOCUMENTS AND TENURE STATUS OF THE PLOT

	Question	Categories	Answer

Q11	What was the legal status of the plot at the time of transfer?	10. Customary land
		20. *Lettre de convocation/bulletin*
		30. *Lettre d'attribution*
		40. Precarious title
		    41.CUH
		    42. CRUH
		    43. CR
		    44. Permis d'occuper
		50. Long-term lease
		60. *Titre foncier* (Ownership title)
		99. Does not know
			/_/_/

Q12	What is the current legal status of the plot?	10. Customary land
		20. *Lettre de convocation/bulletin*
		30. *Lettre d'attribution*
		40. Precarious title
		    41. CUH
		    42. CRUH
		    43. CR
		    44. Permis d'occuper
		50. Long-term lease
		60. *Titre foncier* (Ownership title)
		99. Does not know
			/_/_/

RESULTS FROM A SURVEY OF LAND TRANSFERS   87

| Q13 | What document proves the transfer? | 10. No document
　11. Customary transfer
　12. Noncustomary transfer
20. Authenticated certificate of sale
　21. Customary transfer
　22. Noncustomary transfer
30. Nonauthenticated certificate of sale
　31. Customary transfer
　32. Noncustomary transfer

40. Notarial deed

99. Does not know | /_/_/

/_/_/

/_/_/ |

PRICE OF THE PLOT

	Question	Categories	Answer
Q14	How much was paid for the plot?		CFA _____
Q15	Today, how much would the plot sell for (according to informant)?		CFA _____

EQUIPMENT/SERVICES AND DEVELOPMENT OF THE PLOT

	Question	Categories	Answer
Q16	At the time of the transfer, did the plot have access to water?	10. Yes 　11. Connection to the water network 　12. Well 　13. Other 20. No 99. Does not know	/_/_/
Q17	At the time of the transfer, did the plot have access to electricity?	10. Yes 　11. Direct connection to EDM network 　12. Indirect connection to EDM network 　13. Generator 　14. Solar panel 　15. Other 20. No 99. Does not know	/_/_/
Q18	After the transfer, did the plot gain access to water?	10. Yes 　11. Connection to the water network 　12. Well 　13. Other 20. No 99. Does not know	/_/_/
Q19	After the transfer, did the plot gain access to electricity	10. Yes 　11. Direct connection to EDM network 　12. Indirect connection to EDM network 　13. Generator 　14. Solar panel 　15. Other 20. No 99. Does not know	/_/_/
Q20	Since the transfer, has there been any investment/development of the plot? (multiple answers possible, 3 maximum)	10. Yes 　11. Agricultural investment 　12. Building with permanent material 　13. Fence with permanent material 　14. Well 　15. Other 20. No 99. Does not know	/_/_/ /_/_/ /_/_/

Notes

1. The following communes are covered, with number of observations in parentheses: Baguineda-Camp (255), Bamako commune I (2), Bamako commune IV (5), Bamako commune V (35), Bamako commune VI (30), Bancoumana (28), Bougoula (28), Diago (68), Dialakoroba (39), Dialakorodji (45), Dio Gare (30), Doubabougou (81), Kalabancoro (99), Kambila (51), Kati (26), Mande (141), Meguetan (17) Moribabougou (46), Mountougoula (148), N'Gabacoro-Droit (92), Ouelessebougou (61), Safo (172), Sanankoroba (88), Sangarebougou (21), Siby (23), Tiele (6), and Tienfala (18). Four of these communes are located in Bamako District, 21 in Kati cercle, and 2 in Koulikoro cercle.
2. The differences in development and bargaining power of sellers and buyers could also contribute to the price difference. Table 5.1 surprisingly reports a higher price for land obtained through public authorities than on the noncustomary market. To understand this result, it should be noted that we report raw values that do not take into account differences in plot characteristics, including their location (see the regressions at the end of this chapter), and that median price values can be sensitive to small sample bias (there are only nine observations for public land used for agriculture). It is also not clear whether responses to the questionnaire make it possible to distinguish public allocations from transactions on land acquired from customary landholders to which a precarious title was subsequently issued by a public authority.
3. Note that the questionnaire did not allow for a sufficient distinction between sellers and intermediaries. Some coxers (informal brokers) who appear to be sellers of customary land in survey responses are in fact simply facilitating the transfer of land. Other coxers who rightly appear to be sellers on the noncustomary land market do indeed buy customary rural land that they subdivide for residential use before reselling it. There might also be some confusion in responses regarding the profession of the seller and the function of the person delivering an administrative document or a title within the land administration.
4. With the collected data, it was difficult to distinguish a lettre d'attribution from a lettre de notification (see footnote b in table 3.1, which details the reasons for this ambiguity). For the analysis, all lettres d'attribution are treated as lettres de notification, that is, administrative documents.
5. About 50 percent of agricultural landholders who did not have an administrative document at the time of transfer had a certificate of sale authenticated by the commune (see annex 4A).
6. A plot with an administrative document sold on the noncustomary market may be either of public origin, but sold illegally, or of customary origin, with the buyer having subsequently benefited from regularization of tenure before selling the plot on the noncustomary market (see chapter 3 and figures 3.1 and 3.2 for the procedures; annex 4A for the different documents; and figure 4.2).
7. See Selod and Tobin (forthcoming) for the construction of a theory.
8. The changes depicted in the table are likely to be underestimated because of "right censoring" (because information on tenure after the date of the survey is not

available, by definition). It also aggregates figures for plots that have been held for different periods ranging from less than one year to up to three years.

9. Explanations could be that improving tenure takes too much time to be observed within the retrospective three-year timeframe of the survey, is most likely too costly for many households, or is not always desired. Another possible explanation is that plots in the survey area may not have been affected by a regularization operation between the transfer and survey dates.

10. It is legitimate to do so. Because no specific instructions were given to respondents, the prices they declared are likely inclusive of bribes and should thus approximate the market value of land under the assumption that the agents in the land administration are able to fully capture the difference between administered prices and market prices.

11. Because possible issues of endogeneity cannot be addressed, causality should not be inferred from the results; they should be interpreted as indicative of correlations only.

12. When using prices at the time of the transfer, time dummies are used to account for the year the plot was transferred. When using estimated prices at the time of the survey, we consider the tenure variables at the time of the survey instead of the tenure variables at the time of transfer. All other variables are considered time invariant.

13. The fact that more than half the plots in the whole sample are held under an administrative document could thus be viewed as an indication of the difficulty households face in upgrading to a precarious title or an ownership title.

14. Estimations of price increases with the data are also approximate given that only the year of transfer is available and not the exact date. There may also be inconsistencies in declared prices if some respondents do not include bribes paid in their declaration. Finally, the sample may not be perfectly representative of the whole land market in Bamako and its surrounding area.

15. The last plot was surveyed in April 2012, so a period of 2.3 years was used for the calculation.

References

Durand-Lasserve, A. 2004. "La question foncière dans les villes du Tiers Monde: un bilan." *Economies et Sociétés* 38 (7): 1183–211.

Rakodi, C., and C. Leduka. 2004. "Informal Land Delivery Process and Access to Land for the Poor: A Comparative Study of Six African Cities." Policy Brief 6, University of Birmingham, Birmingham, U.K.

Selod, H., and L. Tobin. Forthcoming. "The Informal City." Policy Research Working Paper, World Bank, Washington, DC.

Wehrmann, B. 2008. "The Dynamics of Peri-Urban Land Markets in Sub-Saharan Africa: Adherence to the Virtue of Common Property V. Quest for Individual Gain." *Erkunde* 62 (1): 75–88.

Chapter 6

Conclusion

Rather than proposing a new set of legal and administrative measures, the objective of this study is to present a framework for a systemic analysis of the land delivery channels and the functioning of the land market. The resulting analysis can help enable decision makers to assess the repercussions on the land market of policy measures affecting any component of the system.

The Relevance of the Method Adopted

Analysis of the land delivery system for housing helps provide a better understanding of the workings of land markets in the urban and peri-urban areas of Bamako and its rural hinterland. This system is the result of interactions between three land delivery channels (which differentiate land by the status of its tenure at the time its use became primarily residential for the first time). These three channels are a public channel with land coming from the state's private domain; a customary channel with land obtained from the descendants of the first occupants who consider themselves to be the owners of the land; and a formal private channel relating to plots with an ownership title. Apart from status at the time of first residential use of the land, each channel is distinguished by the possibility for holders of plots to improve their tenure and sell them on land markets. There are multiple links between the three channels (see figure 4.1) as can be demonstrated by a few examples. A *lotissement*[1] may shift a plot from the customary channel to the public channel, whereas if a formal property developer obtains ownership title to a piece of customary land, that land will move into the formal private channel. Highlighting the channels and the links between them in the land delivery system requires meticulous study of the legal procedures and of actual practices—which do not necessarily comply with those procedures—concerning land transactions on the one hand and tenure status on the other. This information helps the sharp distinction often drawn between formal and informal markets to be overcome and allows the diversity and complexity of situations to be acknowledged (figure 4.2).

Taking account of the interactions between channels in the land delivery system also helps provide a better grasp of the nature of land conflicts. Conflicts may arise between holders of customary rights who have allowed use of their land and the *commune* (administrative jurisdiction headed by a mayor) that engaged in a lotissement operation on this land; conflicts may also develop between occupants of plots purchased from customary holders and a formal property developer that says he has an ownership title covering those plots.

Unequal Household Access to Land for Housing

Analysis of the delivery channels for residential land also suggests different possibilities for inhabitants to access land in accordance with their employment status and incomes. Private sector employees who work for formal companies may access plots through the intermediary of their employers; public sector employees may obtain plots through housing cooperatives; public and private sector employees as well as other persons with medium and relatively high incomes can access social housing at affordable prices; and people with high incomes, whatever their status, can purchase plots from formal property developers. Plots to which these categories of households have access come under the formal private channel and have ownership title; they were, to begin with, allocated or sold by the state on advantageous terms to land and property development companies and housing cooperatives. Households with access to these plots represent only a small proportion of inhabitants.

Other households generally purchase plots directly from customary rights holders, or on the noncustomary market (chapter 5); they may subsequently benefit from a lotissement or regularization operation and, in principle, obtain a document from the communes giving them the right to apply for a precarious title. To exercise that right and therefore improve tenure status, the minimum requirement is to pay local development taxes and undertake various formalities; once obtained, the precarious title may still not be recognized if the plot is in an unauthorized lotissement. All these elements, along with the possibility of obtaining a sum of money that is often destined to cover expenses they cannot pay out of their income alone, lead a good number of holders of such plots to sell them, although doing so is not authorized. The plot may then be purchased by someone who wants to make profits from it. It will not necessarily be used to house the buyer's household; all or part of it may be rented out, usually after the construction of a dwelling unit, or it may be held until its price rises significantly. Speculative demand thus contributes to rising prices on the land market.

It must be pointed out that employment status and incomes are not the only factors that determine the hierarchy of possibilities for accessing land, because social and political networks also play a critical role.[2]

The Results of the Survey of Land Transfers

A survey of land transfers was carried out between February and April 2012 in an area corresponding to the urban and peri-urban areas of Bamako and its rural hinterland. The results provide useful insights into the functioning of the land market.

Two-thirds of the transfers took place in the noncustomary market segment, and in three-quarters of cases on this market, the transactions involved plots with simple administrative documents that can only be granted by the public authorities during lotissement or regularization operations. It thus appears that regularization is not an obstacle to transfers as a large number of these plots are subsequently sold on the noncustomary market by the beneficiaries.

Formal transactions involve slightly more than 4 percent of all plots when considering only plots with ownership title; 16 percent if those with precarious title are added, but the survey does not indicate whether transactions with precarious title complied with all the legal requirements concerning transactions (see chapter 4). The formal market therefore seems to be very limited. It involves plots closer to the city center with the highest prices.

A fifth of the total transfers relate to plots purchased directly from holders of customary rights at the beginning of the customary channel. None of them had an administrative document at the time of the transfers, thus situating them in the most informal part of land markets (figure 4.2). These plots are farther away from the city center and less expensive, on average.

The survey and a series of interviews also show that customary land primarily used for agriculture has gradually been transformed into residential plots. Loans for—and sales of—customary land for agricultural purposes nevertheless continue to be found at a certain distance from the city center. This raises the question of land transfers from customary land holders to the well-off inhabitants of Bamako, an issue tackled in the analysis of the customary channel.

An econometric analysis based on land price data serves to confirm important features of the land market in Bamako and its surrounding area. The price gradient related to distance from the city center shows that a land market focused on Bamako extends into the rural hinterland, on the frontier of the area in which land use is shifting from rural to urban and where nonmonetized customary transfers still occur. The coexistence of different forms of tenure on the land market is reflected in the much higher value of land with ownership title, which is up to six times more expensive than land with equivalent characteristics but no title. Precarious titles represent "intermediate" forms of tenure that also attract a substantial price premium. However, simple administrative documents, which were possessed by the majority of landholders, do not confer any land rights. This suggests that these documents offer much less protection than do titles and that many households have difficulty in improving the tenure status of their plots. The analysis also confirms the strong growth in land prices during the three years encompassed by the survey, which greatly exceeds both inflation and income growth, undeniably leading to increasingly difficult household access to land.

How Have Land Market Issues in Bamako Been Analyzed and Addressed to Date?

The synthesis report of the National Land Convention and *États Généraux du Foncier* of 2008–09 identifies the main constraints and problems that compromise the improvement of land governance in Mali and especially those issues related to access to land (République du Mali 2010). Four main issues have been identified and discussed: the legal, regulatory, and institutional frameworks; the harmonization of state domain management with sectoral development policies; land management tools and procedures; and social participation and capacity building in land administration. It is, to date, the most comprehensive consensual diagnosis of land and tenure issues and policy in Mali. However, it does not identify the structural causes of the problems encountered; their dynamics over time are not addressed in the report, which instead gives a snapshot of land management and administration problems; the relationships and interactions between the sets of issues are not discussed in the report, as if they were independent from one another; for each set of issues identified, the report proposes a series of recommendations (more than 60), but neither their compatibility nor their contradictions are considered, and they are not prioritized according to their relative importance and timing for implementation.

The Obstacles to Improving Access to Land

In Bamako, attempts to improve access to land are severely limited by a number of obstacles, including the following:

- A legal and regulatory framework based on a process for accessing full secure land (through, in principle, the ownership title) that is so selective that the vast majority of urban households is excluded

- Intense competition for access to land among a diverse range of potential buyers who have unequal incomes and social connections, and asymmetric access to information
- A wide gap between rules and practices and, as a result, frequent erroneous assessment by people of the land rights they actually hold
- The state's reluctance to recognize or formalize customary tenure
- The limited capacity of the land administration to deal with the demand for secure tenure or tenure formalization
- Widespread corruption in land administration resulting jointly from the land prerogatives of the state and from the juxtaposition of several land delivery channels with a wide range of tenure rights, together with the coexistence of both market and administration-set prices (that is, prices set by an administrative decision at below-market prices)
- Money laundering generated from illicit transfers
- The underestimation by the state of the social, cultural, and political constraints in their attempts to improve access to land: reforming land management and administration is a highly political matter and technical answers are not sufficient.

It can be assumed that the majority of people who have an interest in changing the legal framework of land management are not able to impose those changes; the majority of people who are in a position to make changes have no interest in doing so.

An Accurate Diagnosis Is a Prerequisite for Making Relevant Recommendations

Scholars and experts have analyzed various modes of access to land, but few attempts have been made to describe the land delivery system as a whole.

This study endeavors to show how the delivery channels and the associated land markets make up a system, which implies that any change in one component of the system may have an impact on the others. Viewing land delivery as a system should make it possible to assess the consequences of land-related policy measures. For example, understanding the land delivery system model helps provide an understanding that increasing public land reserves and reaffirming the land prerogatives of the state do not necessarily improve the supply of land for low-income households, given that plots allocated by public authorities are very often put onto the informal market before tenure formalization procedures have been completed.

Improving Access to Land in African Cities: A Highly Sensitive Issue

Access to land in the urban and peri-urban areas and the rural hinterland of African cities—where poverty levels and population growth are high—is a sensitive issue. The dysfunctions of the land sector hinder investments and economic development and have serious consequences for livelihoods, social peace, and political stability. Inadequate policy objectives and the lack of control over land delivery constitute major threats for governments.

The approach described in this analysis is valid not only for Bamako. The same type of assessment of the situation and dynamics of land markets in other cities in West Africa, which have a common history and share very similar legal frameworks and land administration systems, would permit an accurate understanding of the obstacles to conventional measures designed to make access to land more efficient and equitable.

In a context in which the stakeholders involved in land transactions know that the public policies implemented during the past two decades have failed and in which the gap between households' incomes and the cost of accessing land has continuously increased, elected officials, civil servants, decision makers, and professionals seem powerless. The ineffectiveness stems not only from diverging interests or the lack of adequate tools or political will but also from a poor understanding of the processes to access land and the diversity and complexity of the mechanisms and the dynamics of the land delivery system. This study intends to improve the understanding of such complexity in order to overcome the current obstacles and provide more inclusive access to urban land.

Notes

1. The term lotissement is often misused. According to Decree No. 05-115 of March 9, 2005 (which establishes the procedures for carrying out the different types of urban development operations), a lotissement is "the subdivision of a single piece of bare land into plots with appropriate provision of infrastructure and collective facilities to host the buildings to be erected by the future occupants." According to the decree, the lotissement requires the prior issuance of an ownership title, the approval of the regional director of urban planning and housing, and the authorization of the governor of the region or of the district for Bamako. Infrastructure and collective facilities are specified as "roads, drains/sewers, water supply, electricity and telephone." Field work conducted for this study showed that both residents and the authorities use the same word lotissement as a catchall term that refers to a wide range of land subdivisions. There are six types of lotissements

(see chapter 3): (1) customary lotissements; (2) prefectoraux ones (both (1) and (2) are unauthorized, on land that is customary in origin); (3) lotissements by communes following a regularization operation; these are authorized if the commune has an urban planning document approved by the state; (4) unauthorized commune lotissements; (5) private authorized lotissements; and (6) private unauthorized lotissements.

2. It must be recalled that this study does not analyze the situation of tenants and people accommodated free of charge, who constitute half the population of Bamako District and, for the most part, belong to the most disadvantaged population categories.

Reference

République du Mali. 2010. "Rapport de Synthèse des Concertations des États Généraux du Foncier, Ministère du Logement, des Affaires Foncières et de l'Urbanisme, Commission Nationale d'Organisation des États Généraux du Foncier." Bamako, Mali.

Index

Boxes, figures, notes, and tables are indicated by b, f, n, and t, respectively.

increases in urban land prices, 6
lotissement announcement, effect of, 32
of noncustomary vs. customary
    market, 71
precarious title and, 80
private development companies
    setting prices, 37
regressions, 79–82, 79–82*t*, 83*f*
related to distance from city center,
    71, 80, 93
residential vs. agricultural land, 80
land surveyors, 28, 59–60
land tenure systems, 1, 5, 24–26. *See also*
    land delivery channels
security, factors for, xxii, 23, 45*n*10, 95
status of plots at time of transfer,
    73–77
survey results on, 78–83.
    See also survey results of land
    transfers
tenure conversions, 77–78, 77–78*t*
land transfers, xxii. *See also* survey
    results of land transfers;
    *specific types of land and land
    delivery channels*
characteristics of, 71, 72*t*
distance from city center and, 75–77,
    75*t*, 76*f*
profile of sellers and buyers by transfer
    category, 71–73, 73*t*
sales of customary land, 26–28
spatial segmentation of, 69–73
types of, 69–70, 70*f*
Law 02-008 (February 12, 2002), 37*b*
laws, decrees, and other texts on land
    and tenure
civil codes from colonial period, 1
Decree No. 00-274/P-RM (June 23,
    2000), 47*n*24
Decree No. 02-114 P-RM (March 6,
    2002), 46*n*17
Hamidou Diabaté Law (December
    2011), 52
Land Code *(Code Domanial et
    Foncier)*, 25, 60

Law 02-008 (February 12, 2002), 37*b*
    list of, 40–41
lease-to-purchase arrangements, 35
Leclerc-Olive, M., 32
Leduka, C., 7
lending system, 5, 37*b*
lessons learned, 16
lettre d'attribution, 31, 45*n*6, 51, 88*n*5
    multiple *lettres d'attribution* for the
        same plot, 51–52
lettre de notification, 33, 46*n*16, 88*n*5
literature review, 7–8
lotissement
    announcement of, effect on land
        prices, 32
    customary land and, 26
    definition of, 45*n*5, 64*n*1, 96*n*1
    households benefiting from, 92
    informal, 27
    number of unauthorized, 46*n*15
    prefectoral, 27–28
    purpose of, 91

M
Magassa, Hamidou, 4*b*
Mali, description of, 4–5, 10*nn*14–15
Malian expatriates, 5, 38, 73
Mamaribougou-Dollarbougou (Mandé
    commune), 61*b*
merchants as landowners, 5, 29, 77–78
methodology of the study, xxi, 7, 15–20.
    See also survey results of
        land transfers
exclusions from study, 7, 10*n*13
participants, 19–20*n*2
qualitative and quantitative
    approaches combined, 7, 17
relevance of, 91–92
study area, 17–19, 20*nn*4–5
systemic approach to land delivery
    channels and land markets,
    15–17
middle-income groups, provision of
    social housing for. *See* social
    housing program

private property development companies
and cooperatives, 31, 34, 35–38,
47nn23–24, 60
professional associations, 38
protests of "land victims," 3, 60, 63b
public and parapublic land delivery
channels, xxi, xxii, 21, 29–35, 36f
administrative allocation of residential
plots in authorized *lotissements*
and lotissements with
regularization, 31–33. *See also*
regularization operations
administrative documents
associated with, when sold on
noncustomary market, 89n7
formality of sale, 55, 56f
planning documents, preparation of,
46n14
procedures and costs of formalization,
xxii, 44t
sale of public land to private
development companies, 34
social housing program, 34–35.
See also social housing program
spatial pattern of transfers, 70, 70f
types of, 29–30
public-private partnerships, 35
purpose of the study, 6, 91

Q

qualitative and quantitative approaches
combined, 7, 17

R

Rakodi, C., 7
recommendations, 95
reasons people have no interest in, 95
regularization operations, 28, 29,
31–34, 92
remittances, 5
resettlement programs, 3, 26, 31–32, 33,
46n18, 53b, 60, 61–62
results from survey of land transfers.
See survey results of land
transfers

right of way, plots located on, 51
rural hinterland
characteristics of, 19, 19t
customary land in, 25–26
large tracts, sale of, 27
sale of customary land in, 26–28, 94
rural migration to Bamako, Mali, 4, 4b

S

Samé neighborhood, 32
Sanankoroba commune, 32, 59
Save Our Neighborhood (Sauvons notre
Quartier) program, 3, 9–10n9,
31–32
secondary formal market, 38
Sénou-Plateau commune, 63b
short-term credit system, 5
SIFMA property development
company, 61b
social connections and political
patronage, 3, 8, 26, 33, 35, 45n4,
52–54, 53b, 77–78, 92, 95
social housing program, 31, 34–35, 47n22
social unrest and instability due to
inequality in land access, 2–3.
See also protests
Sokonanfing village, 61b, 62
Soro village, 46n11, 65n3
speculators, xxii, 5, 11n17, 26, 32, 34, 73, 92
spontaneous settlements, 31
stakeholders
costs of services provided by,
59–60, 59b
role in land delivery system, 3, 55–59
types of, 55–59, 57–58t
state ownership. *See also* public and
parapublic land delivery
channels
allocation of land with ownership title
by the state, 62–63
gifts of land with ownership title by
the state, 38
presumption of, 1
sale to private property development
companies, 34